Coming Forth by Day

Sissel Kardel

Crosby Street Press

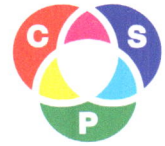

Pyramid, like a mountain evokes stability in form.

Pyramids were originally covered with a facing that reflected the sun in all its brightness, appearing brilliant like a flame or like the sun that sustains us.

It is hypothesized that ancients used pyramids like a mandala to remember that which is greater than the individual and also of the individual.

The pyramid represents the self, the house of hidden places harmony of form. It has an interior.

"I was a hidden treasure who longed to be known" – Koran

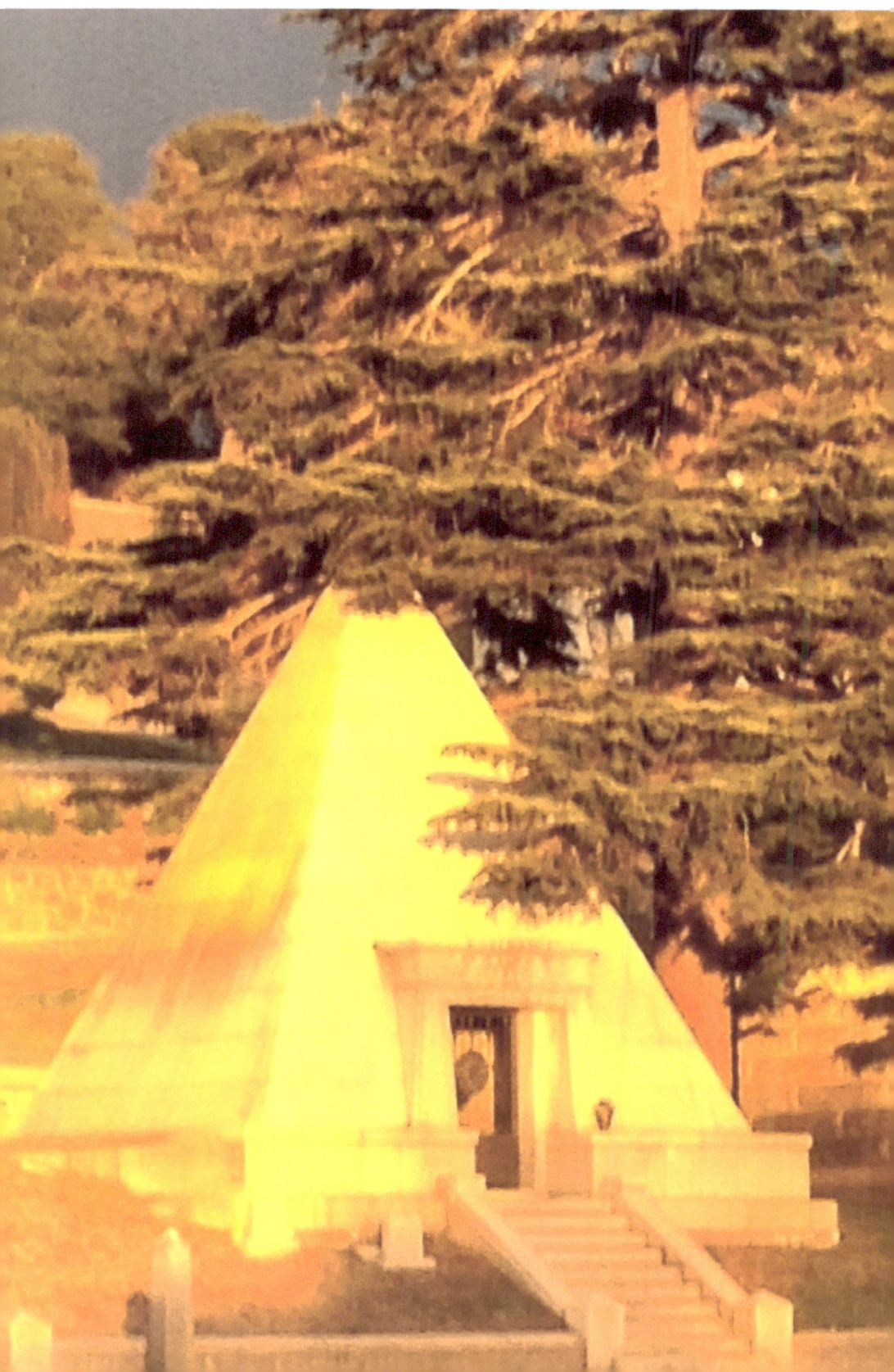

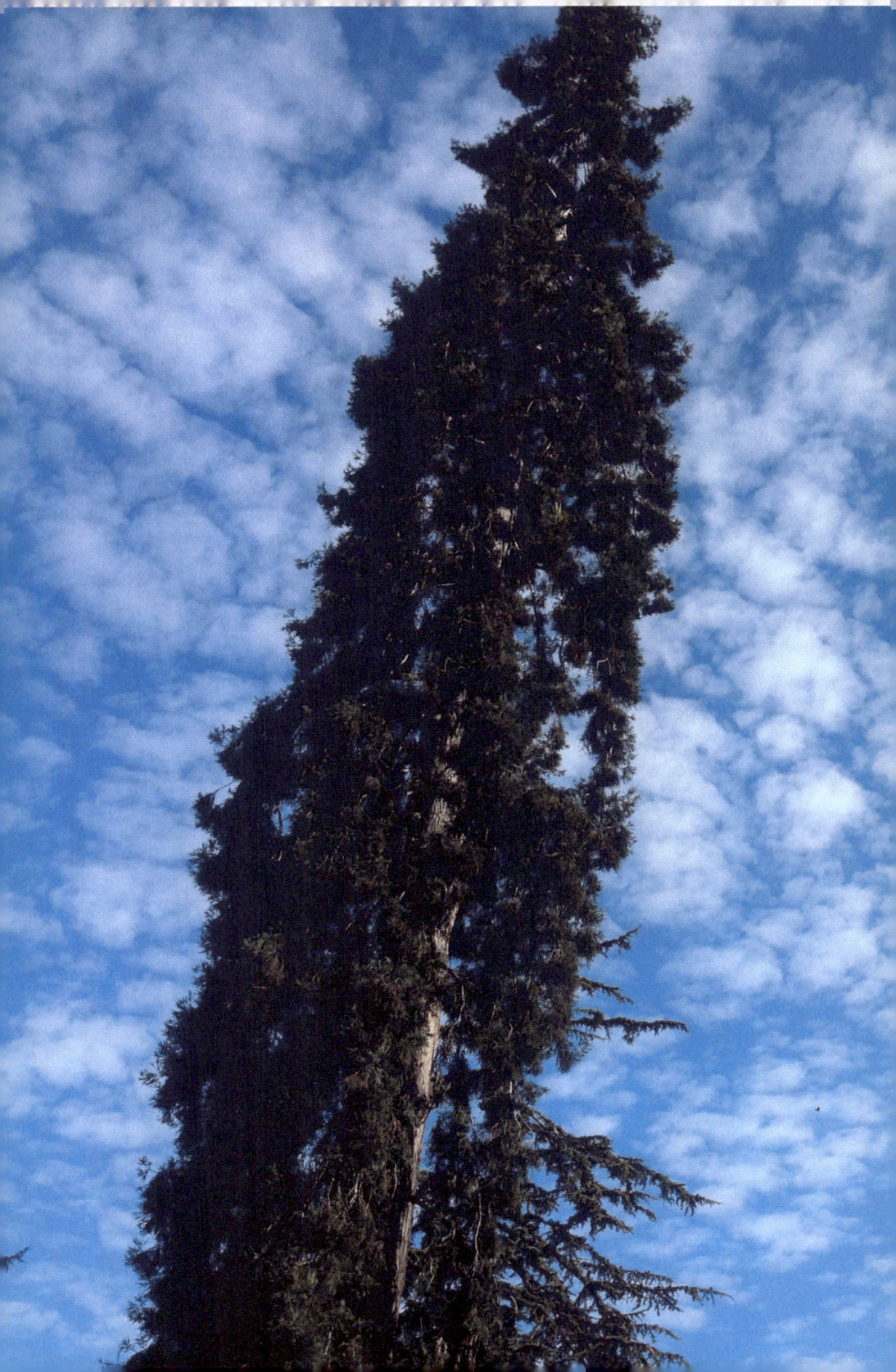

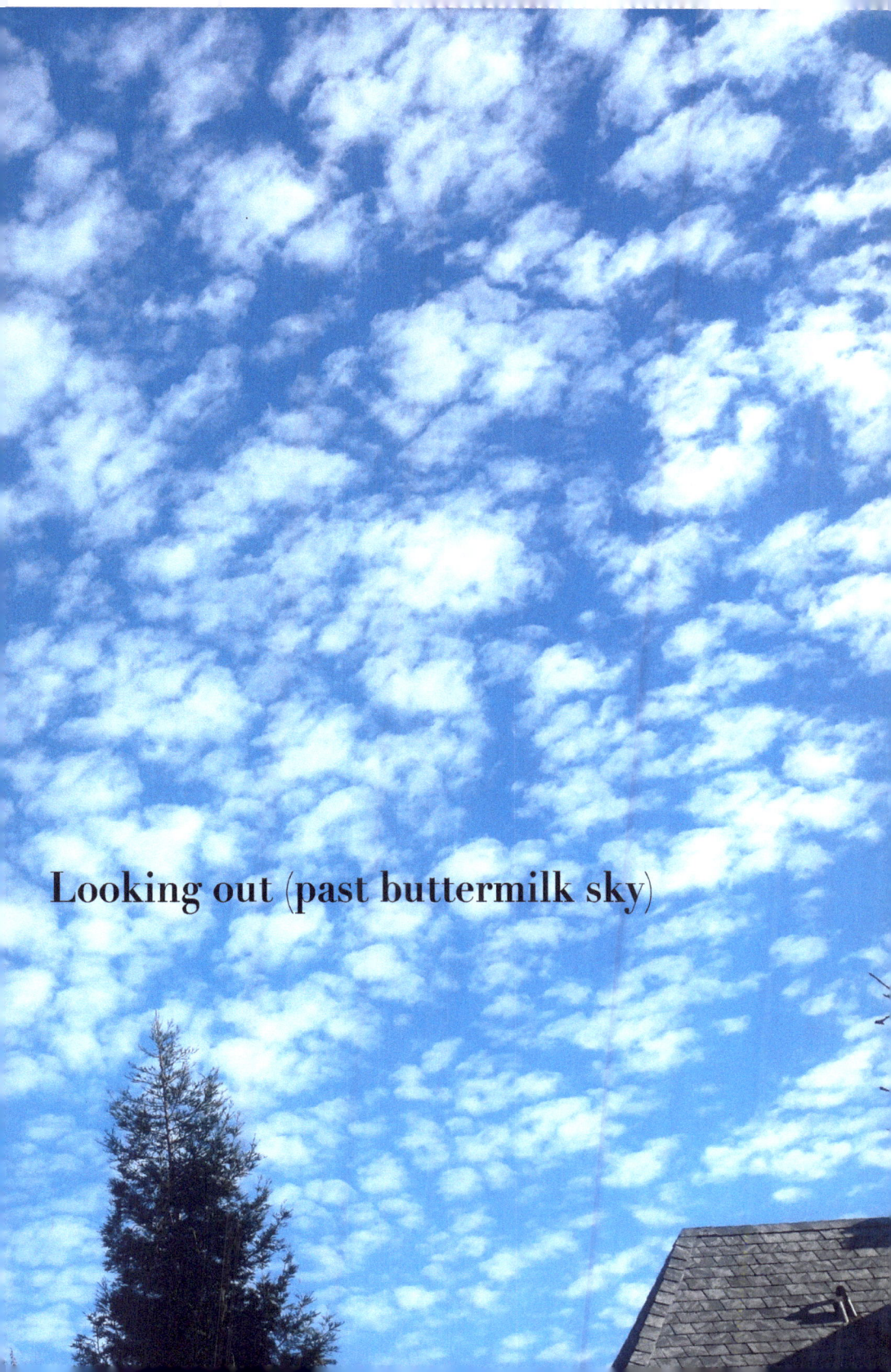

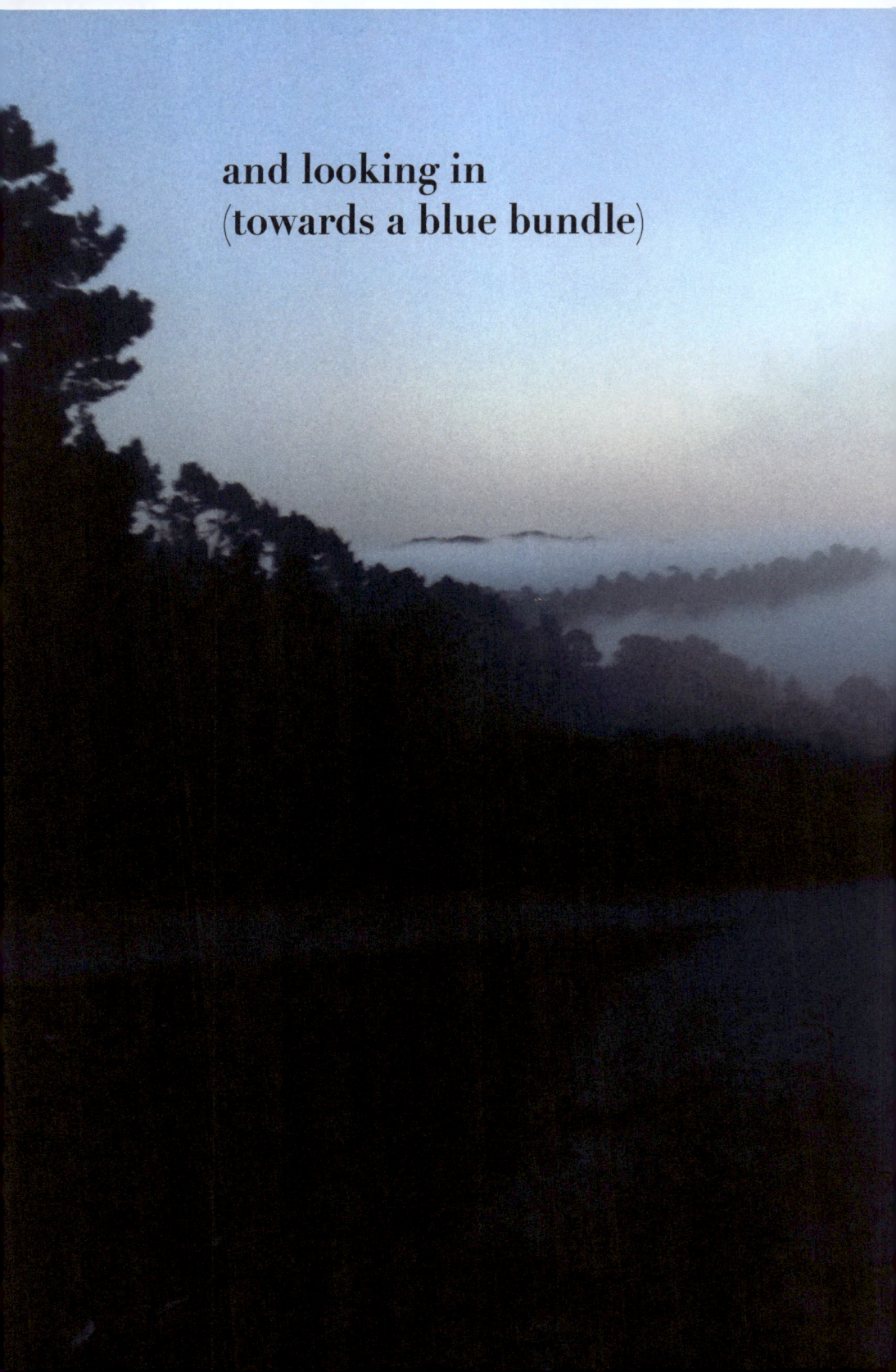
and looking in
(towards a blue bundle)

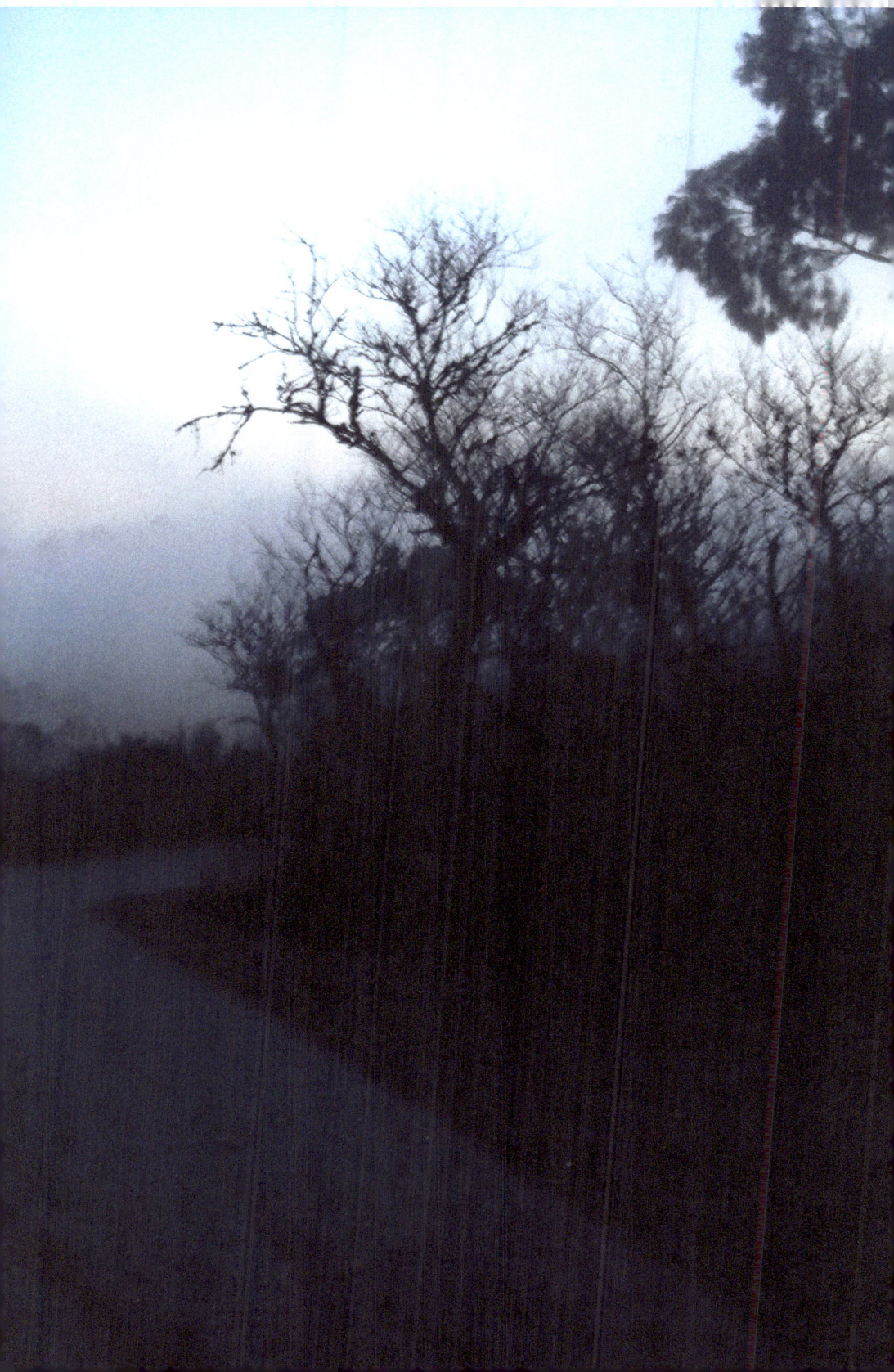

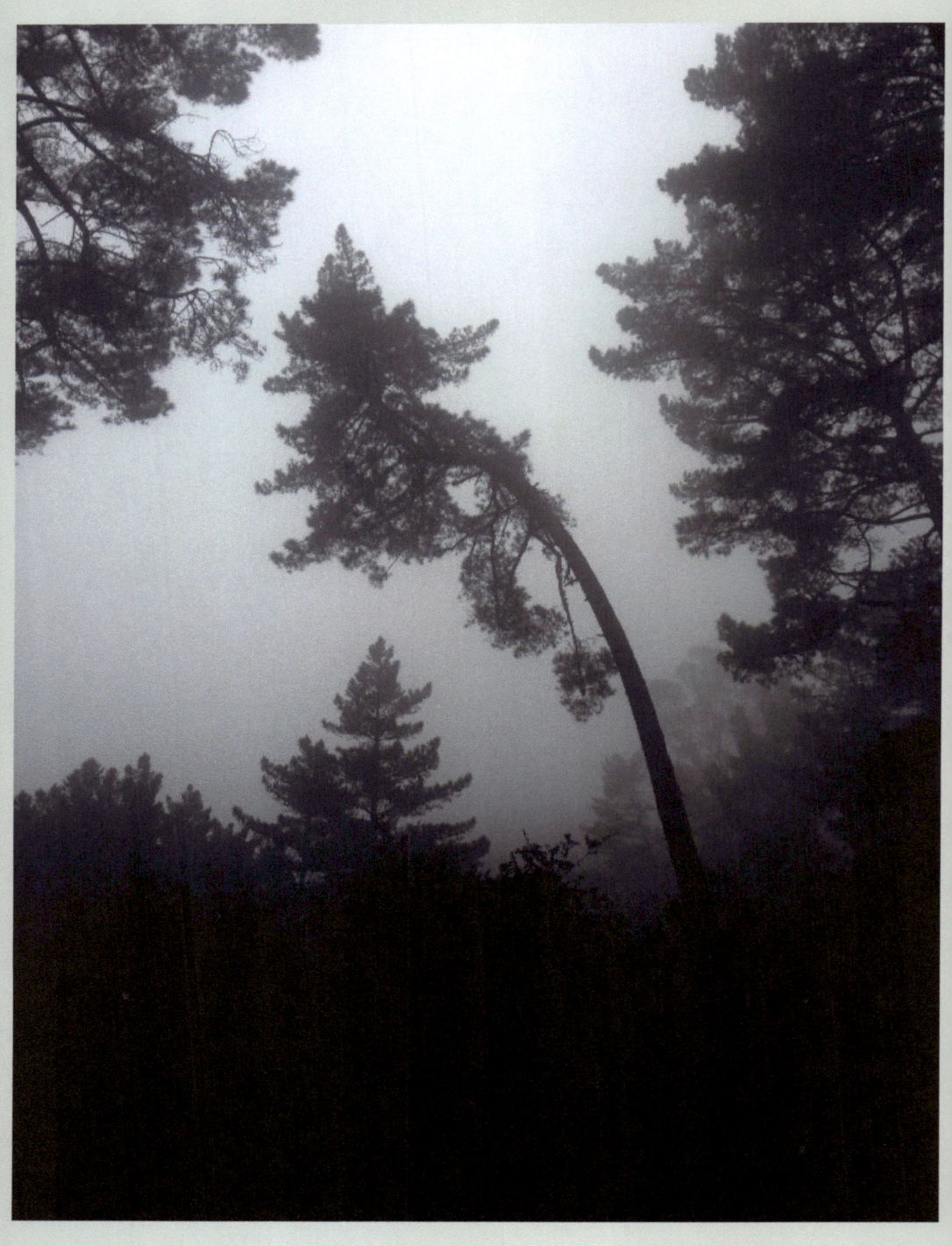

you, the wave, we are plants ascending:
the dizziness of things you have not said

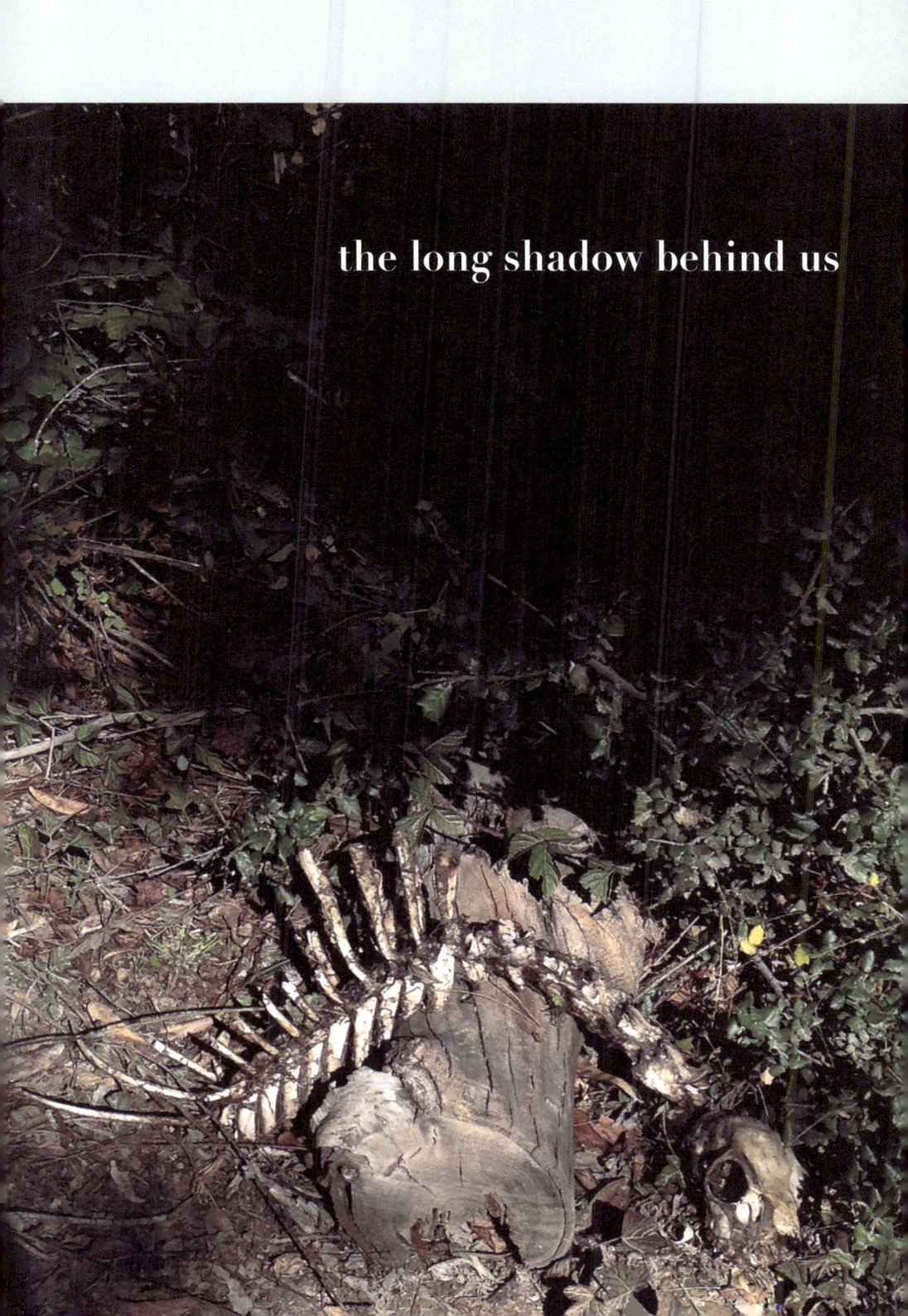

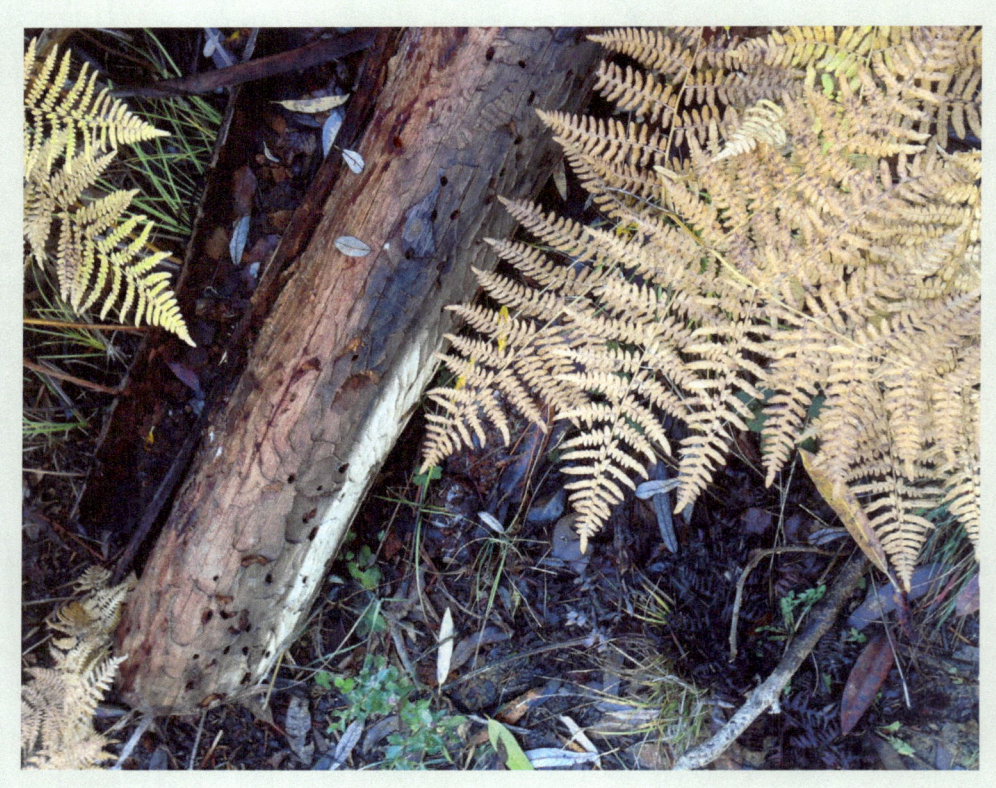

yellow fern and the golden spring

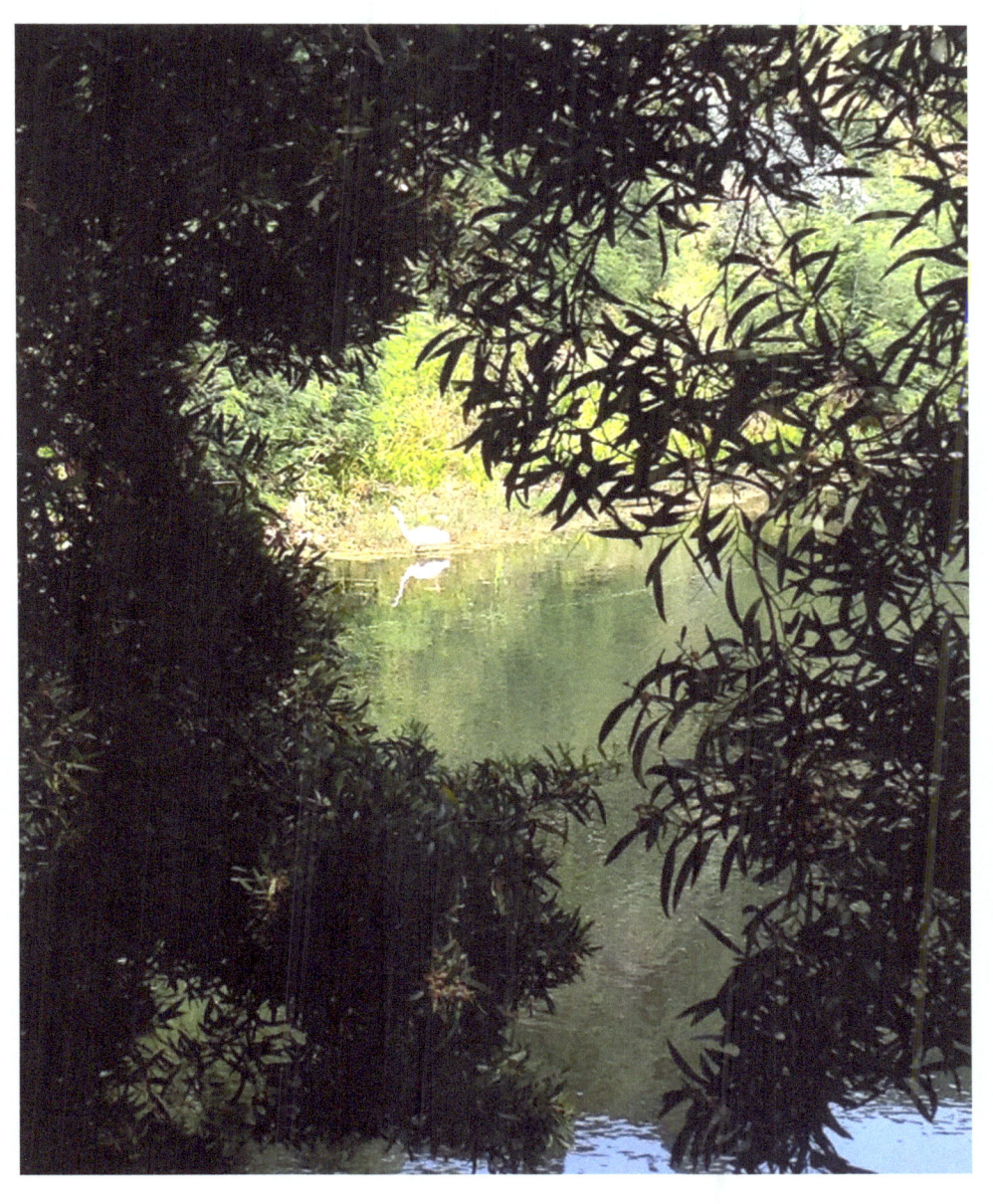

a house of hidden places

sun fed and biting through

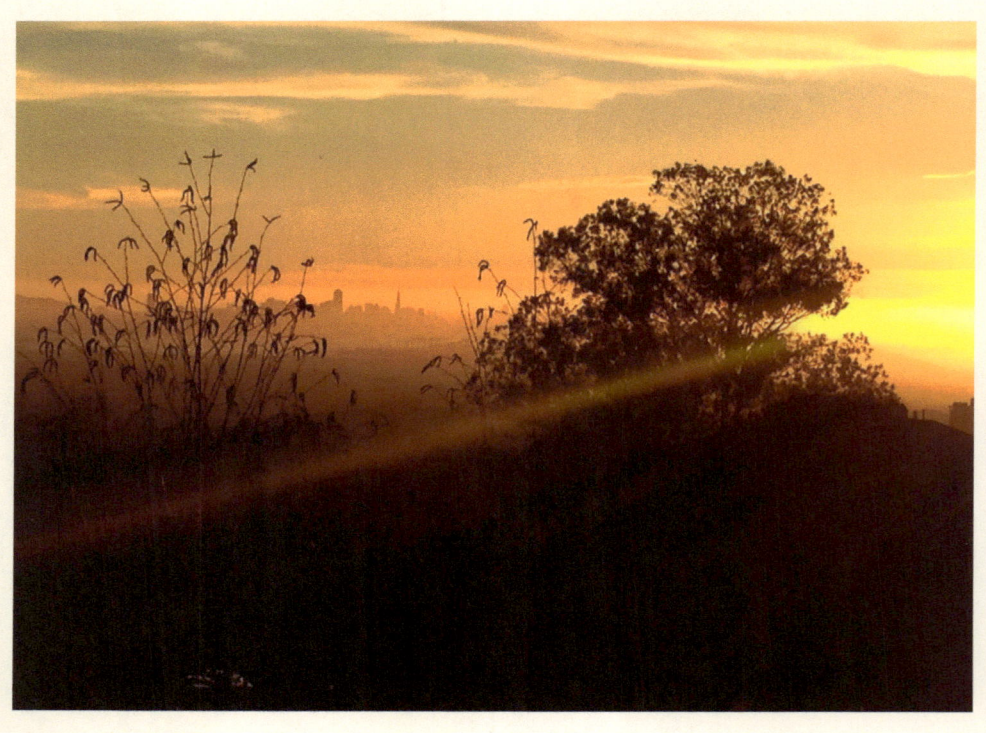

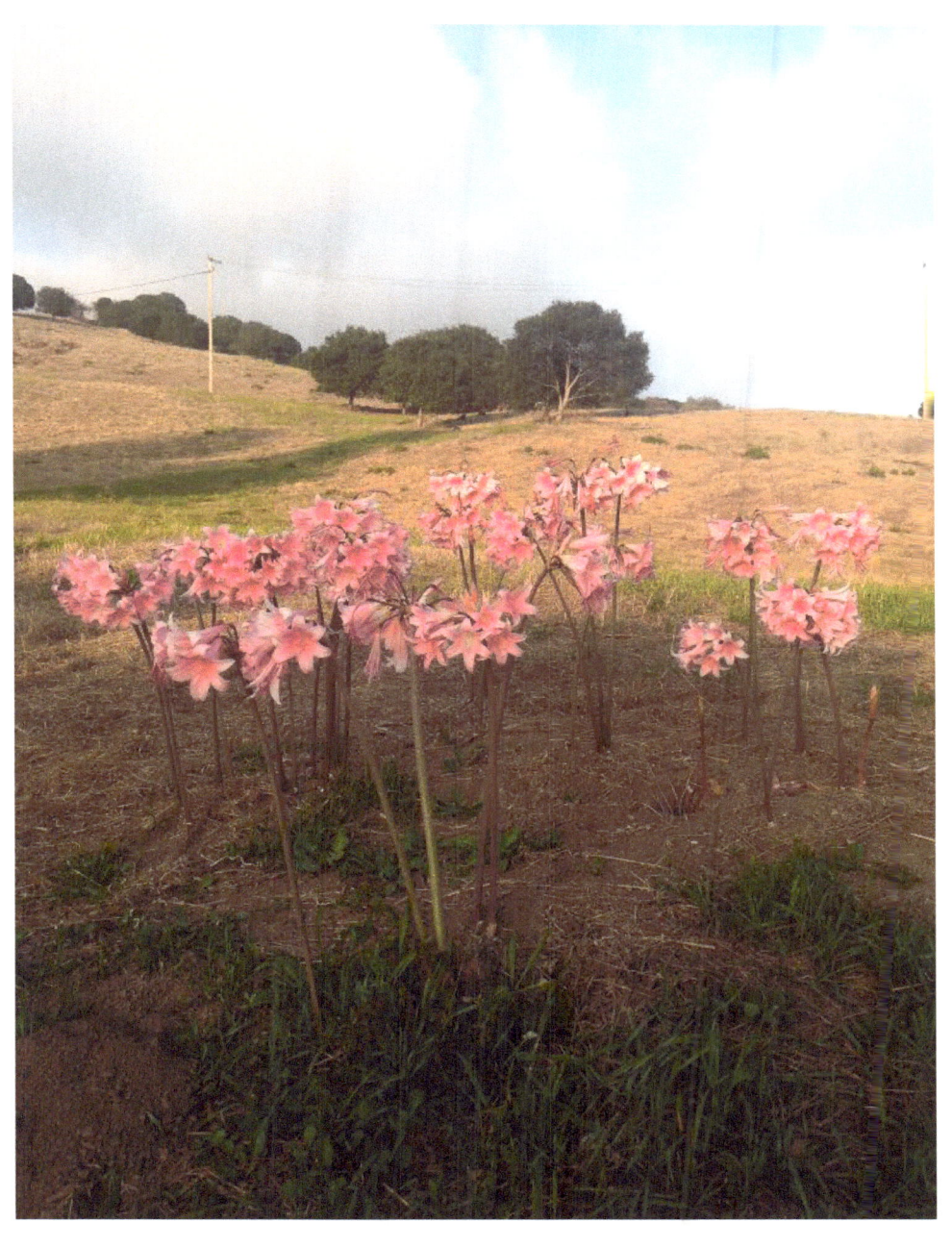

and dropping knees to naked ladies pink

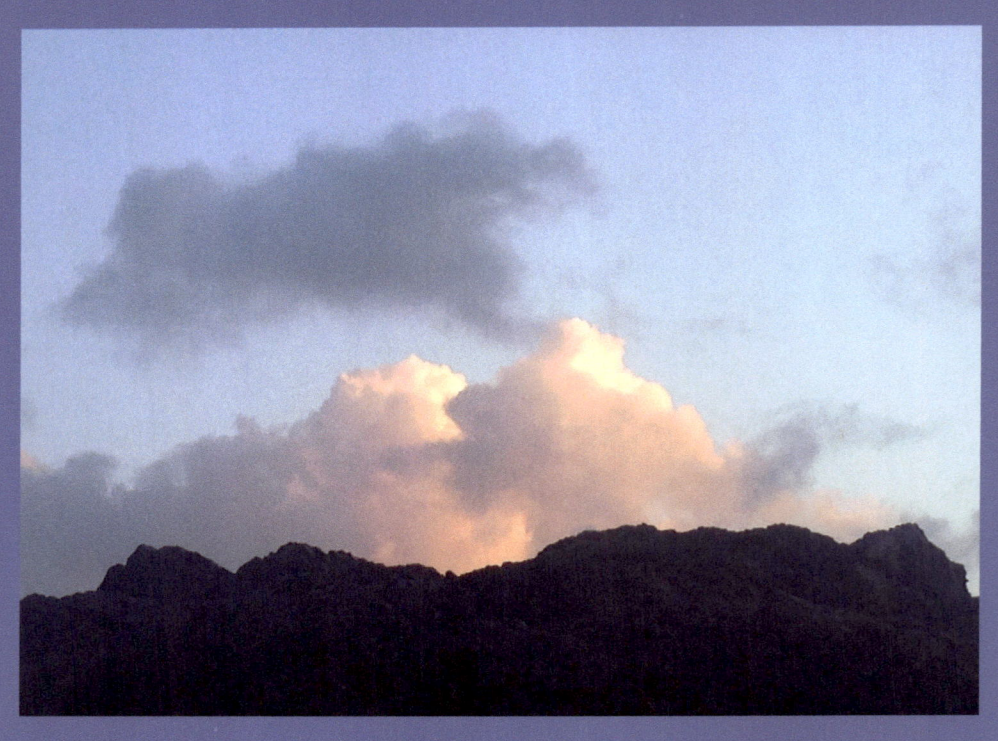

past and future anchor in the nourishing dark

take a mouthful of dark

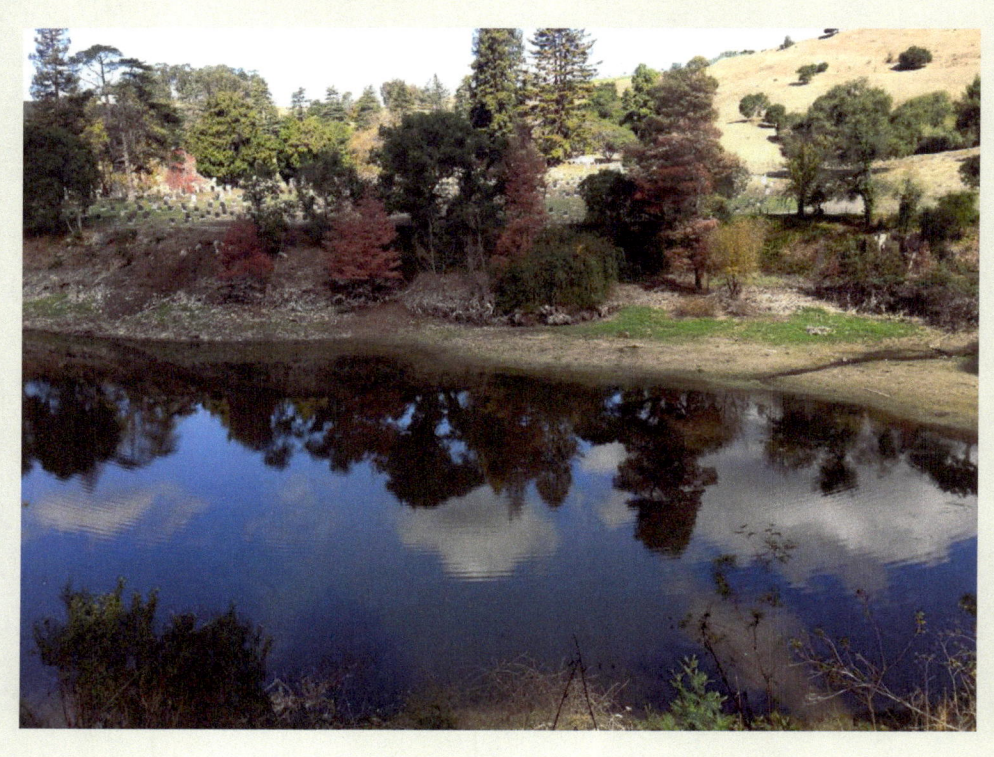

the water appears (bucket by bucket)

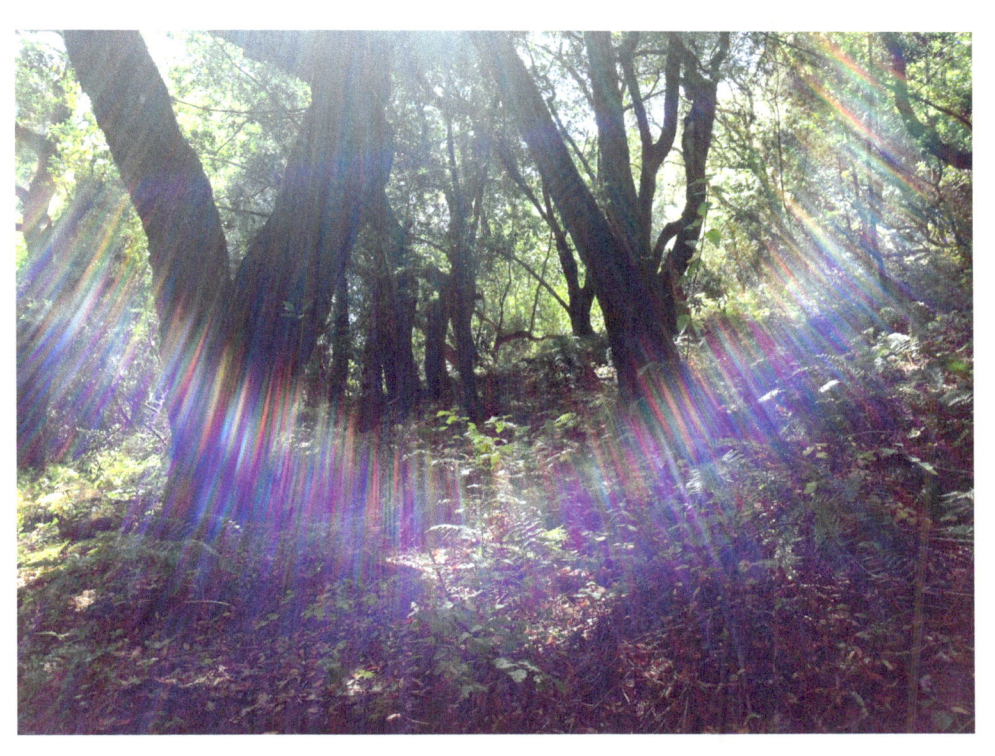

this fragrant place

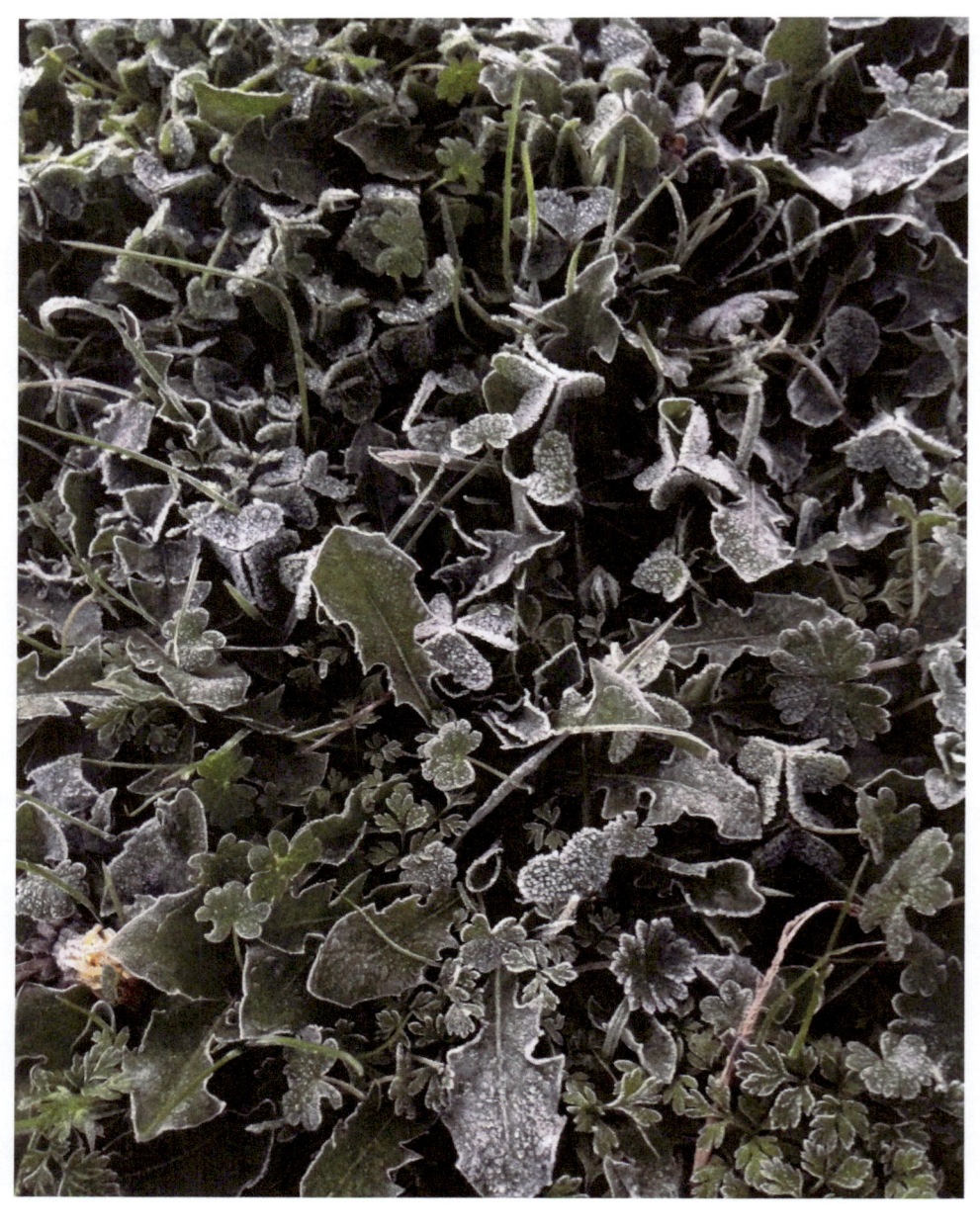

cool ground's lace

magnetic fields illuminate, the only cure

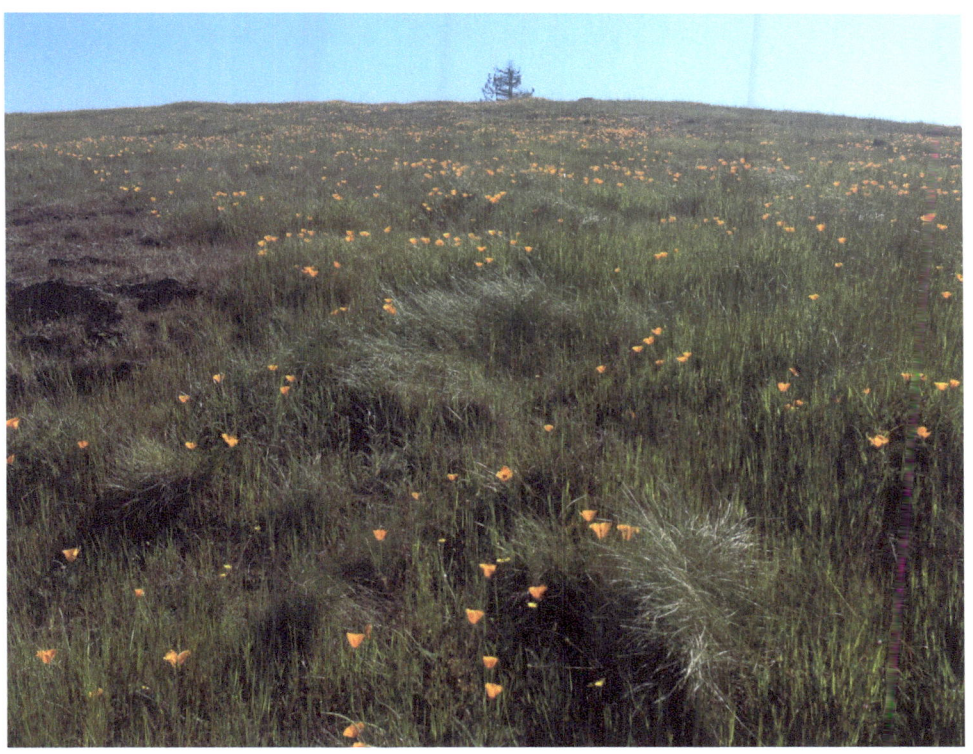

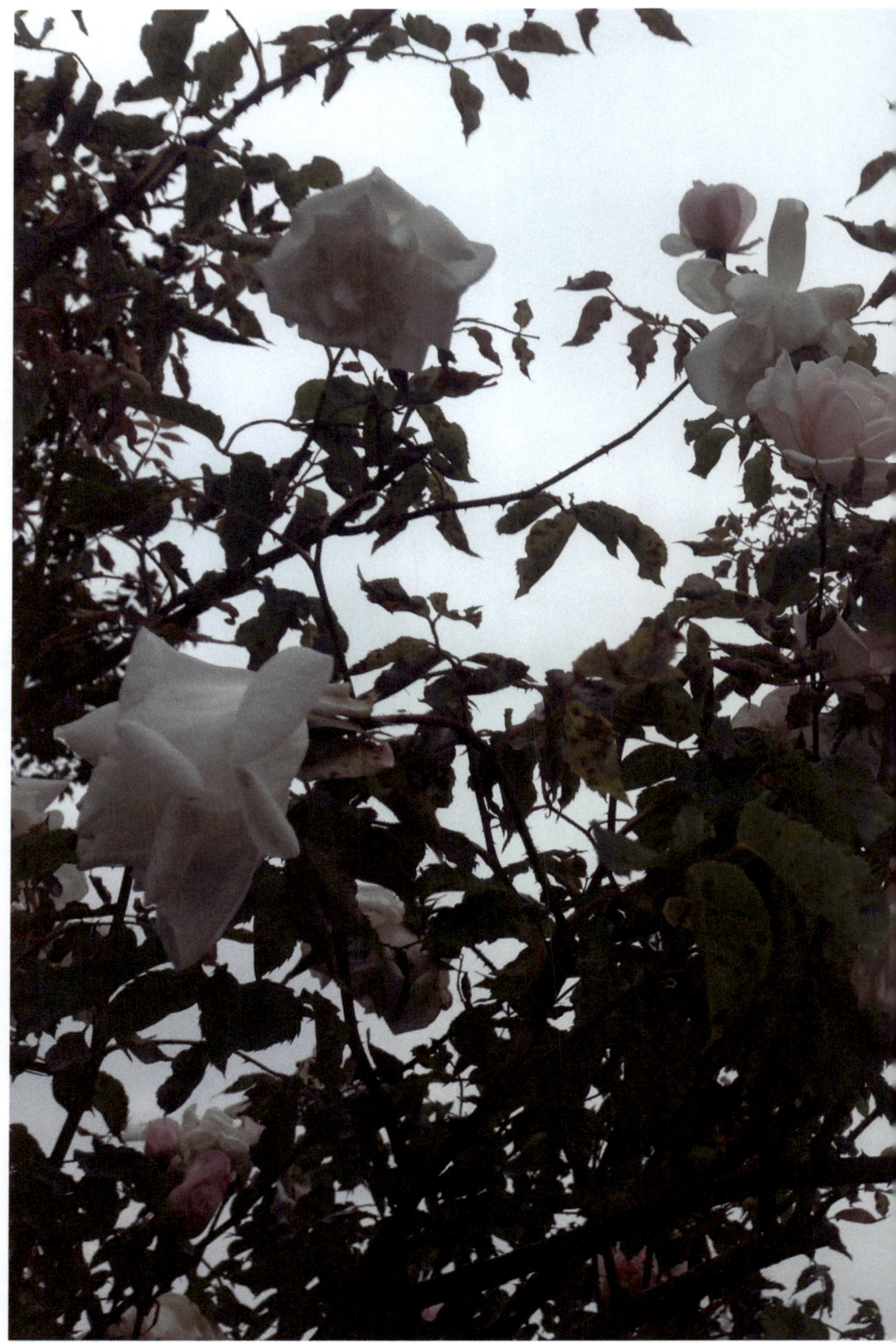

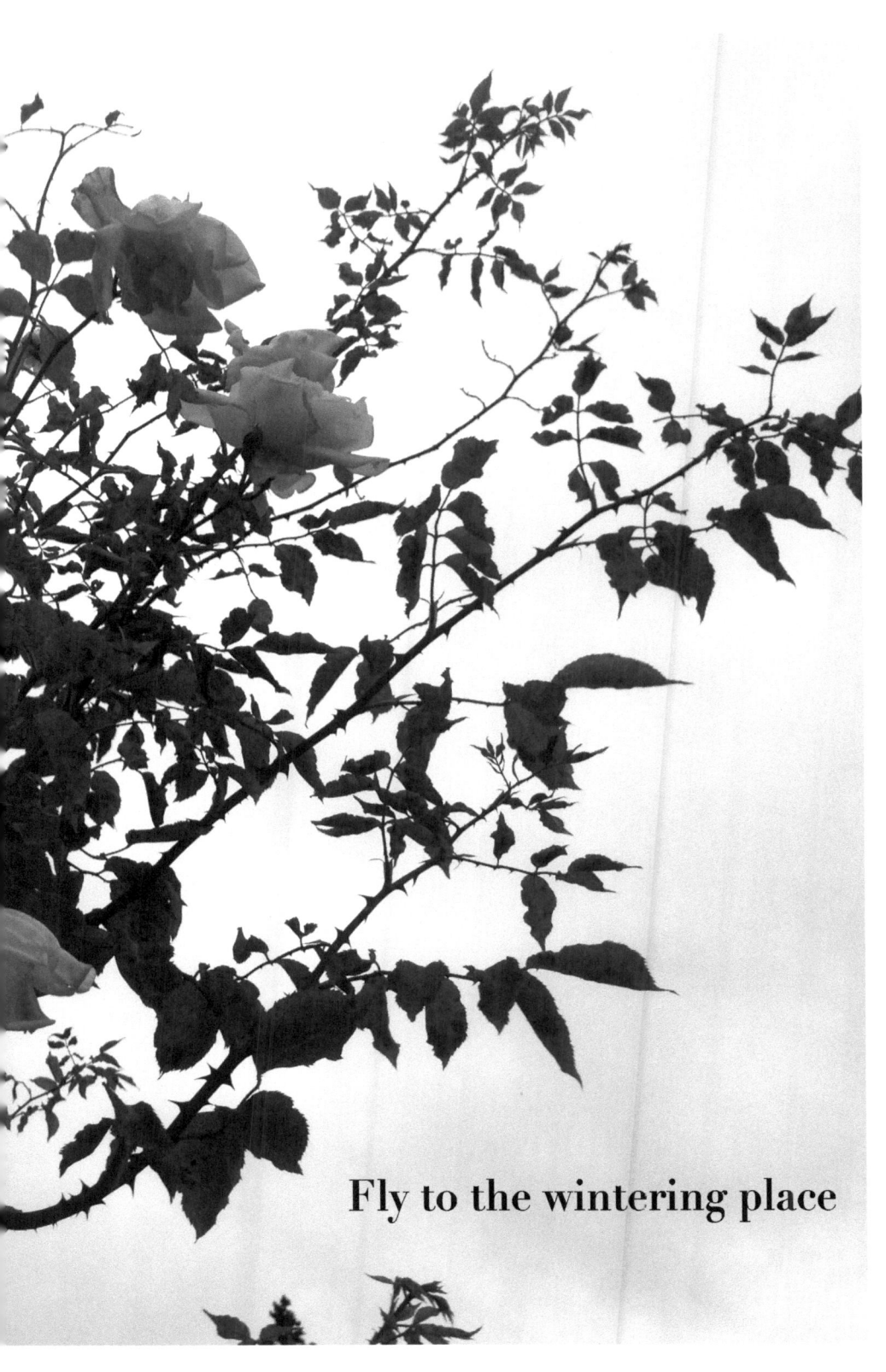

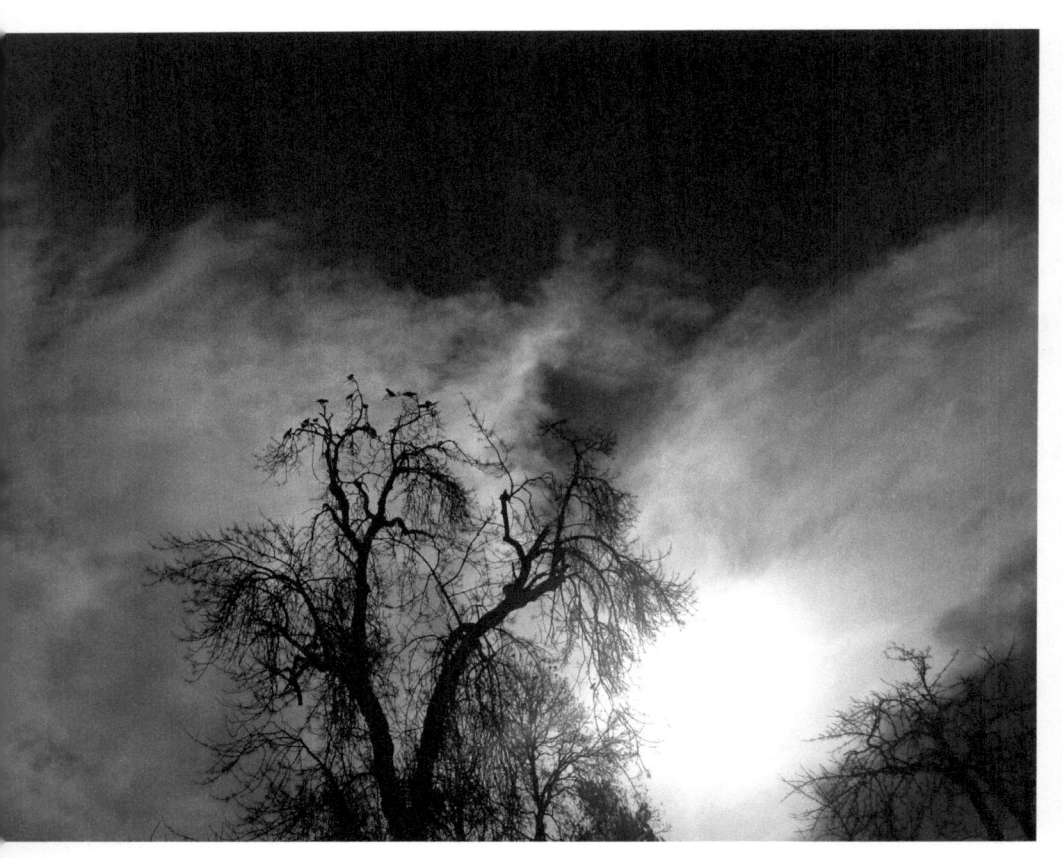

Lay at the roots of a crows' tree

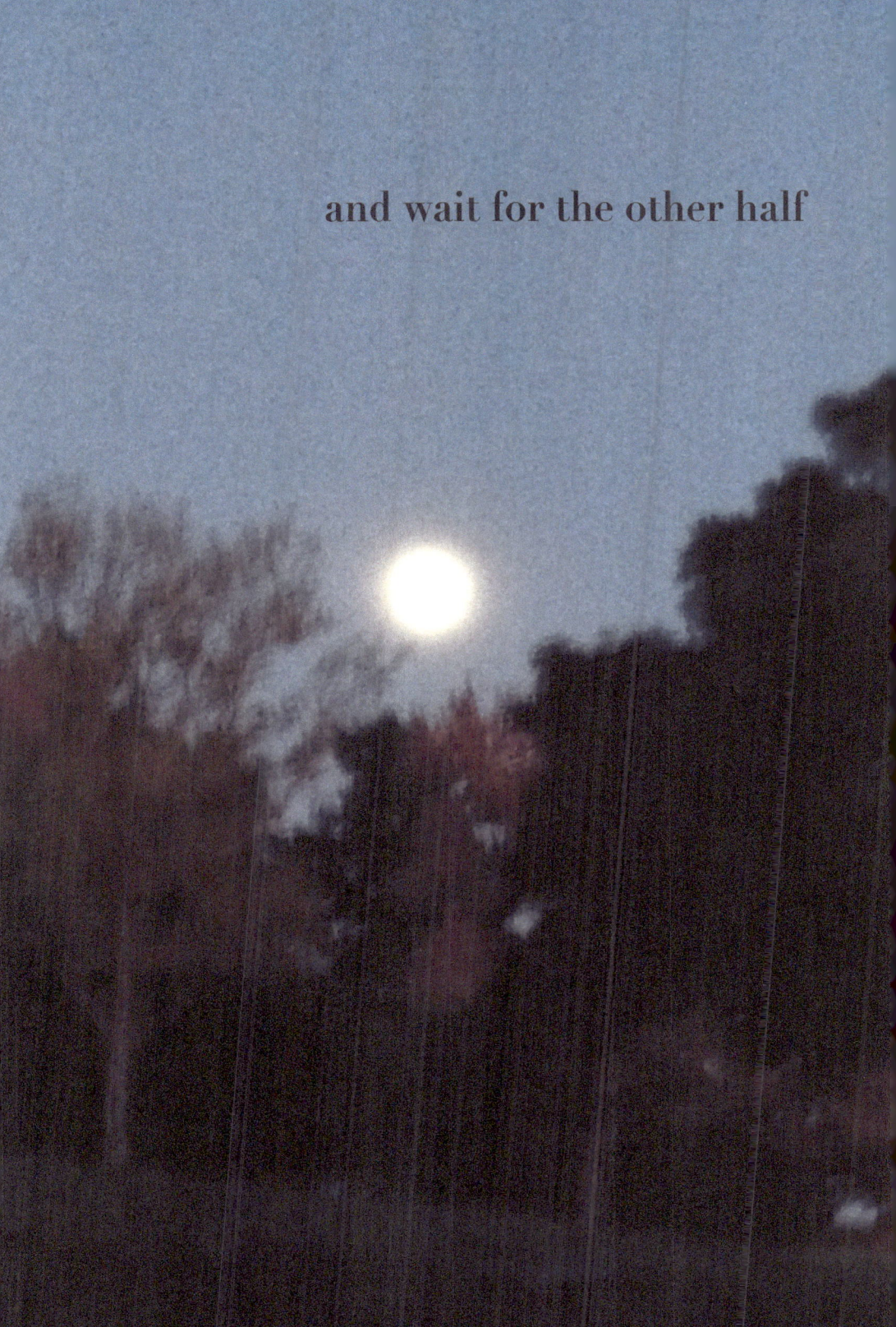

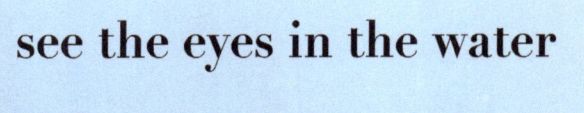

see the eyes in the water

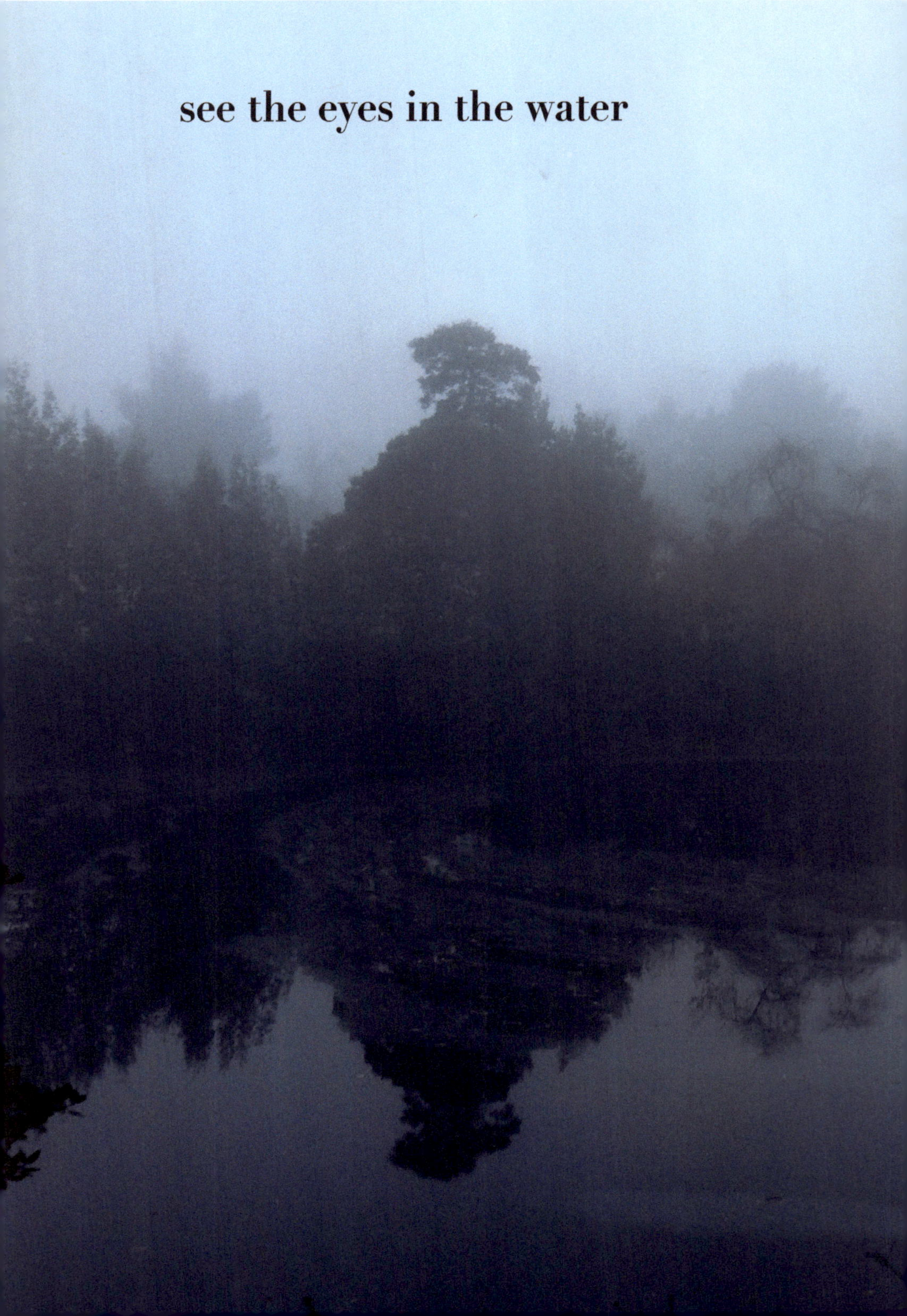

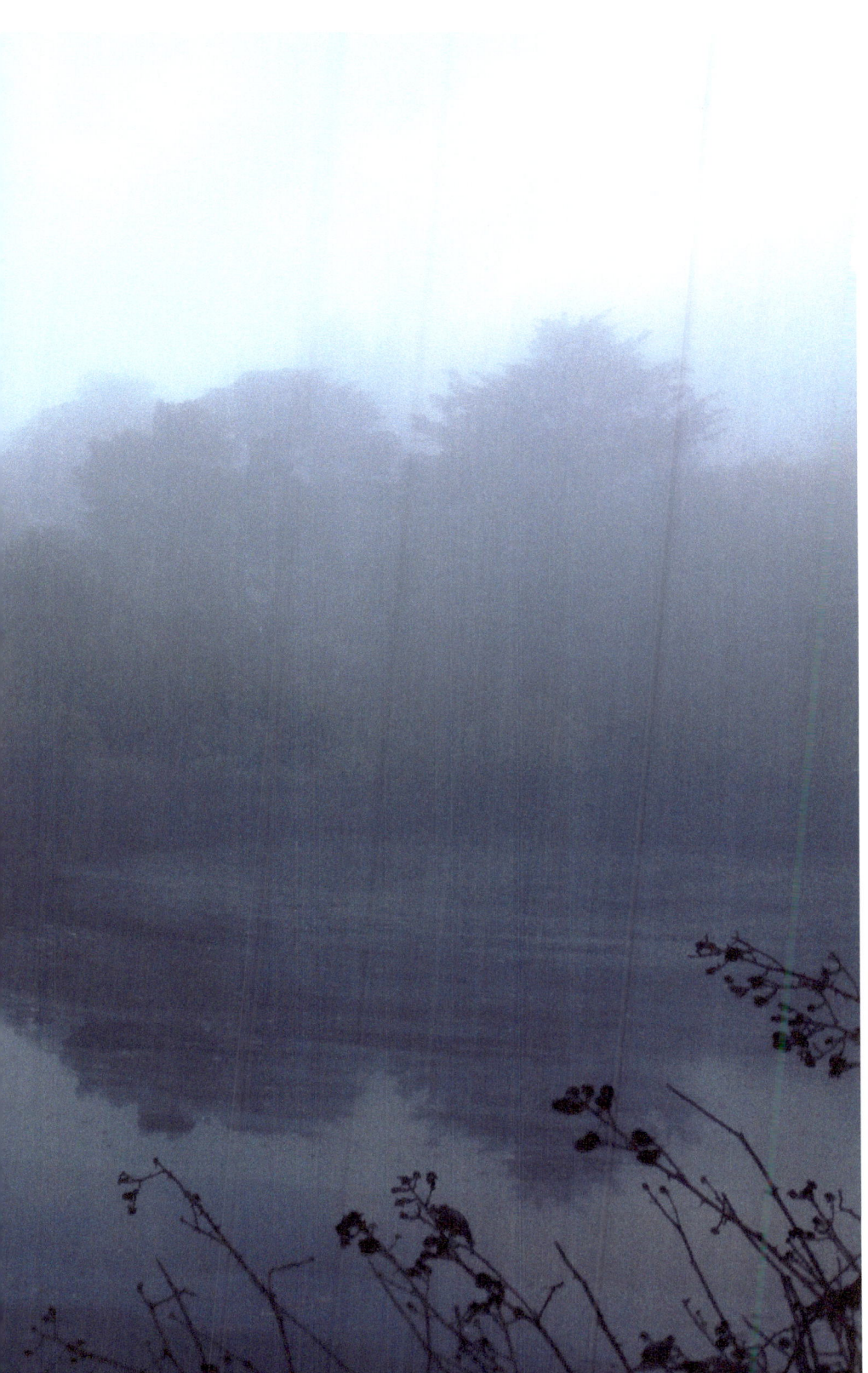

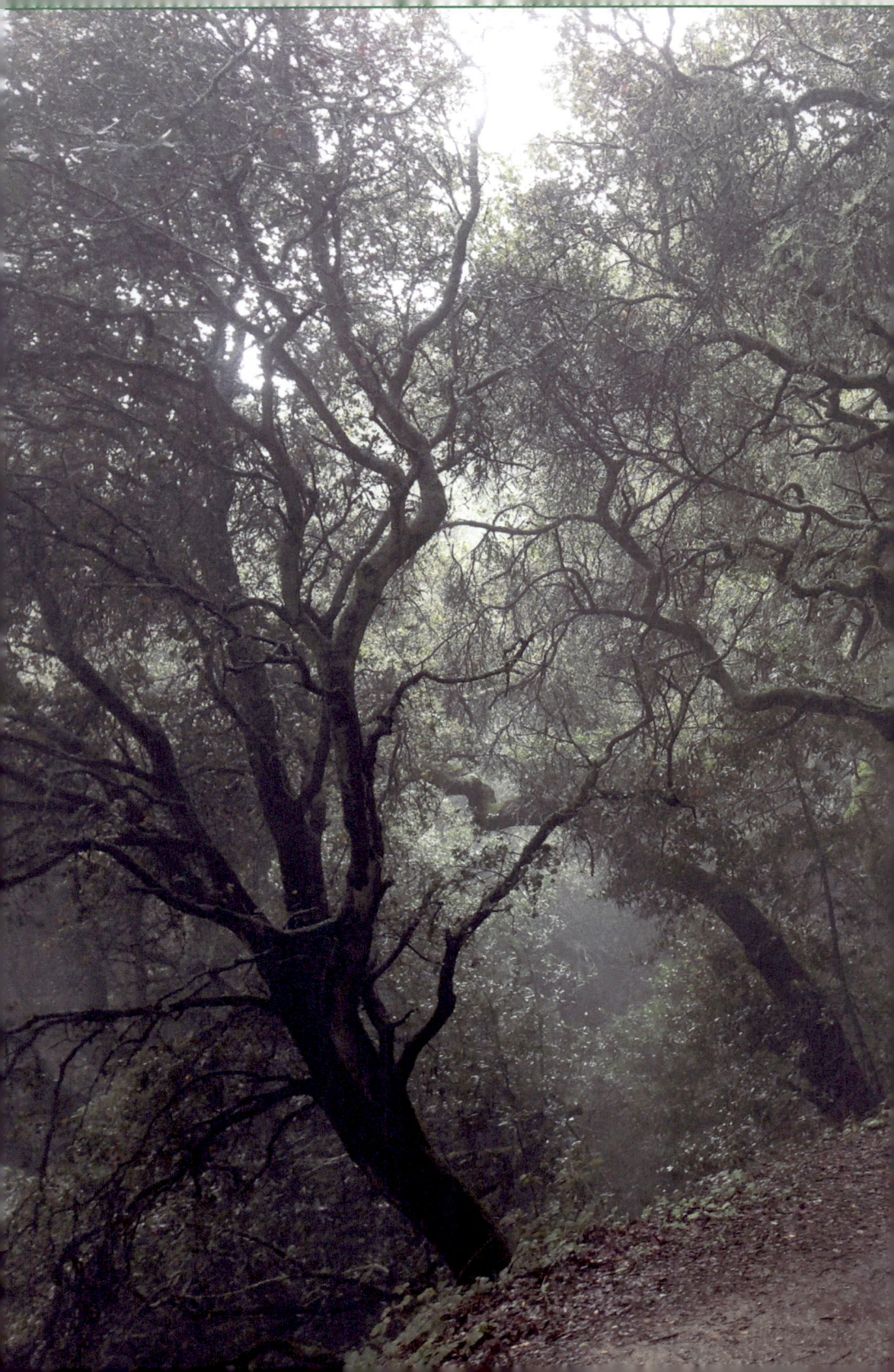

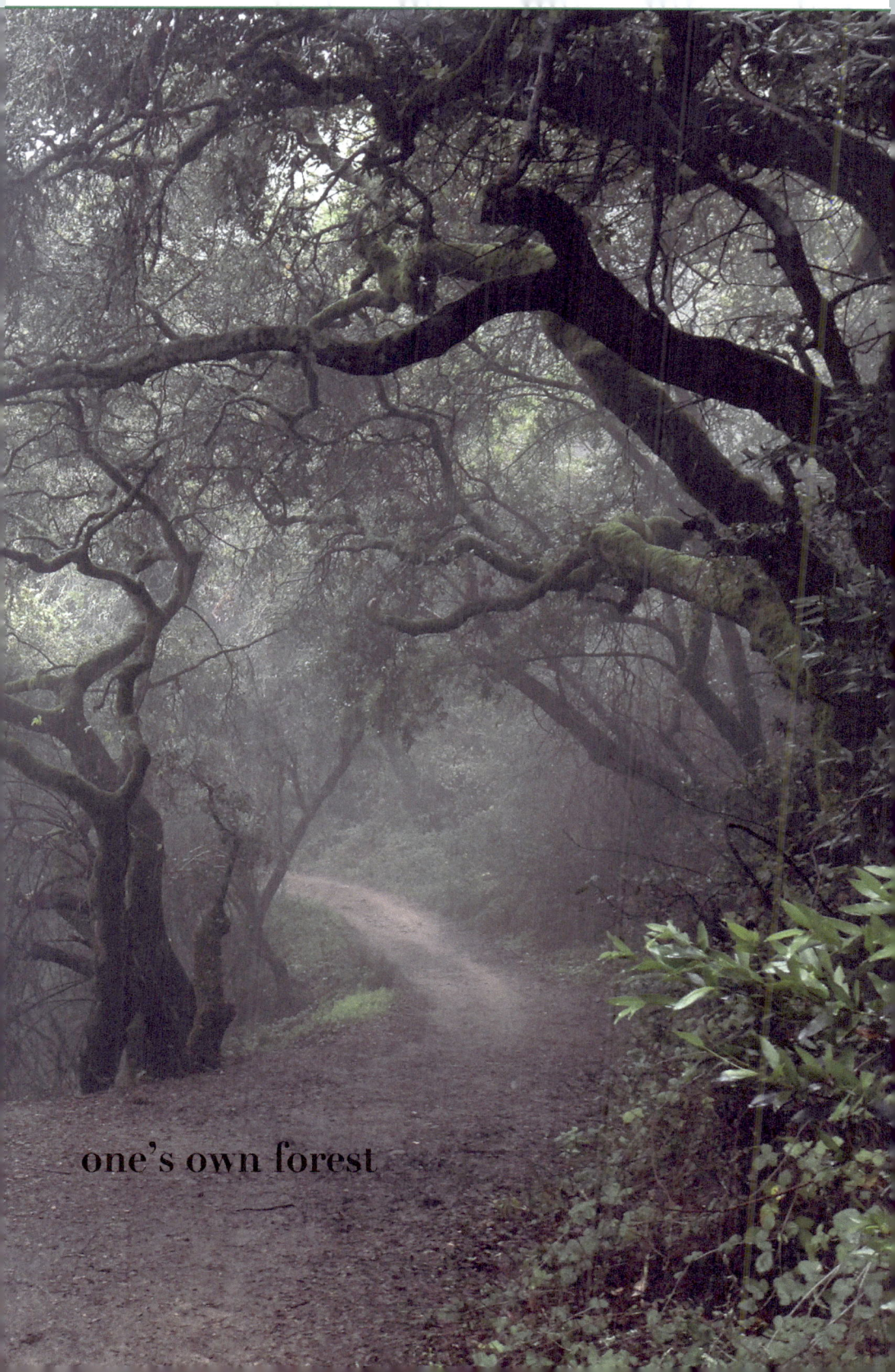

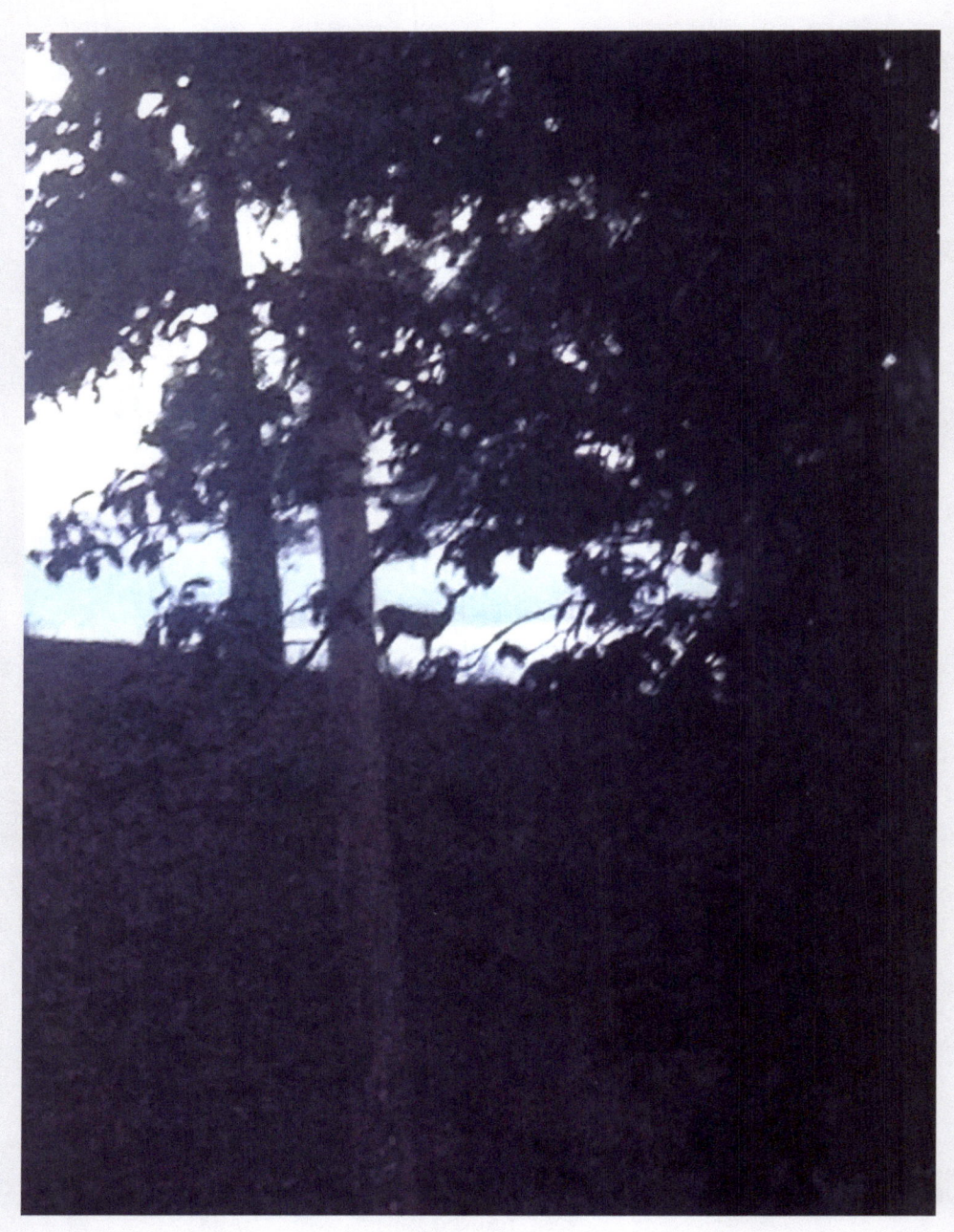

an image at dusk

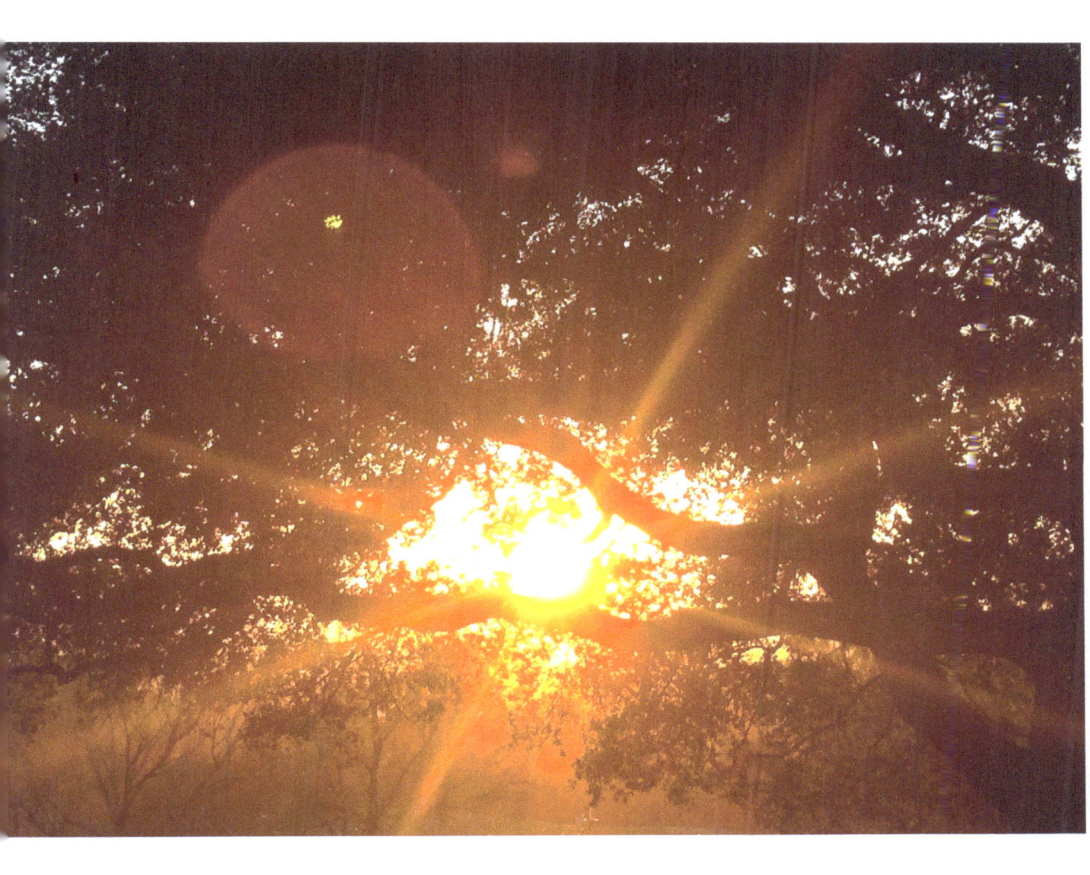

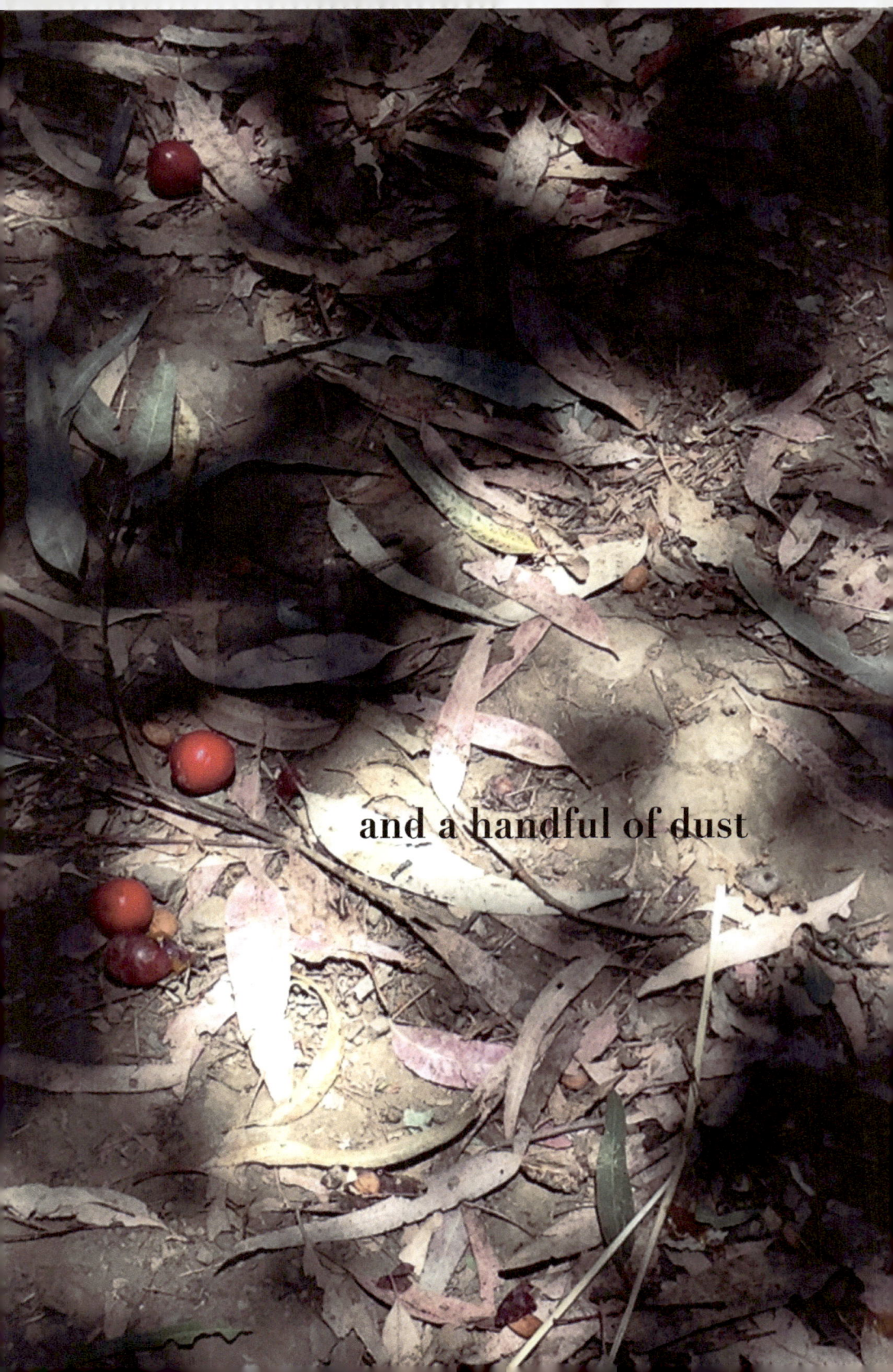

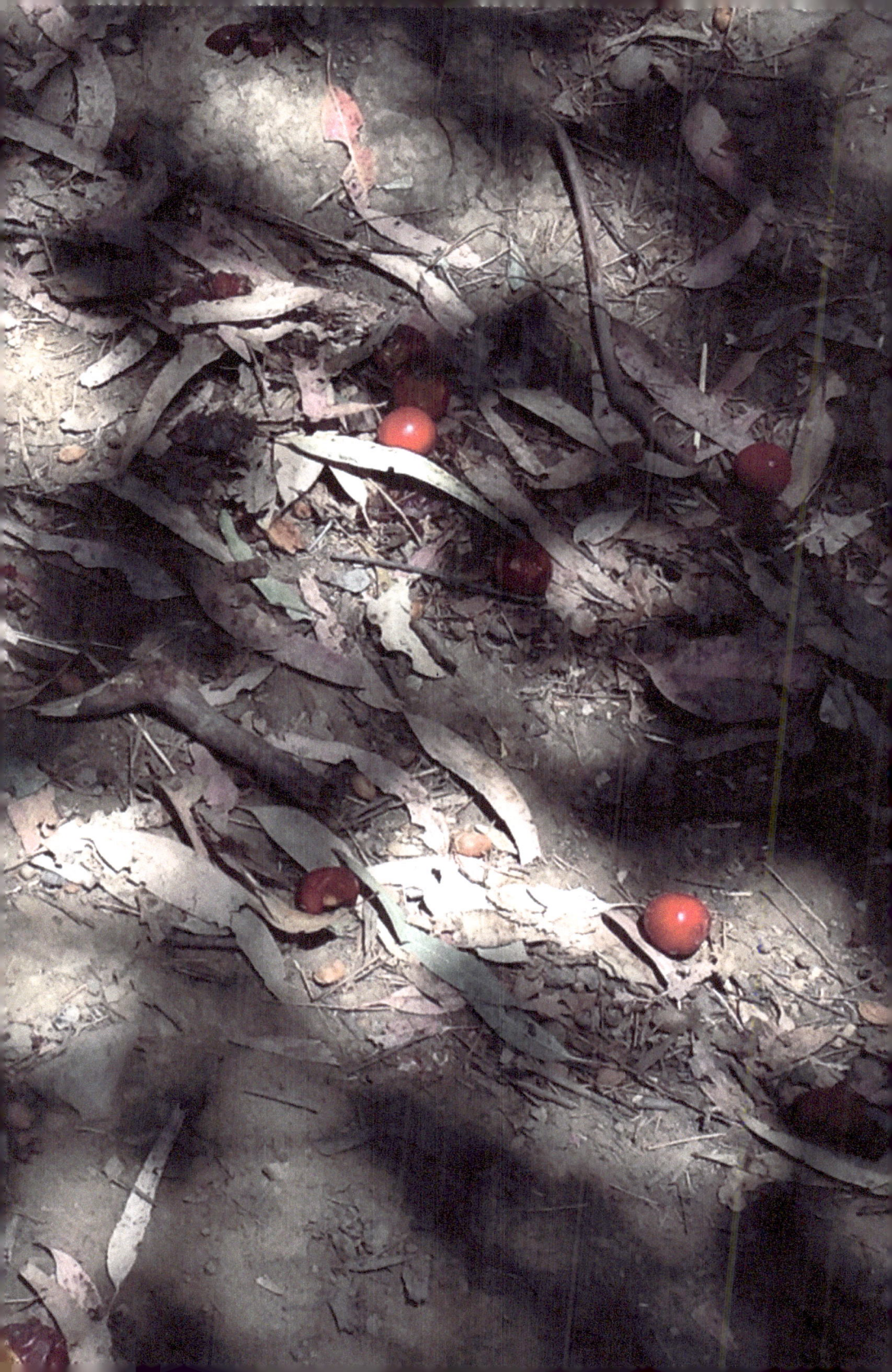

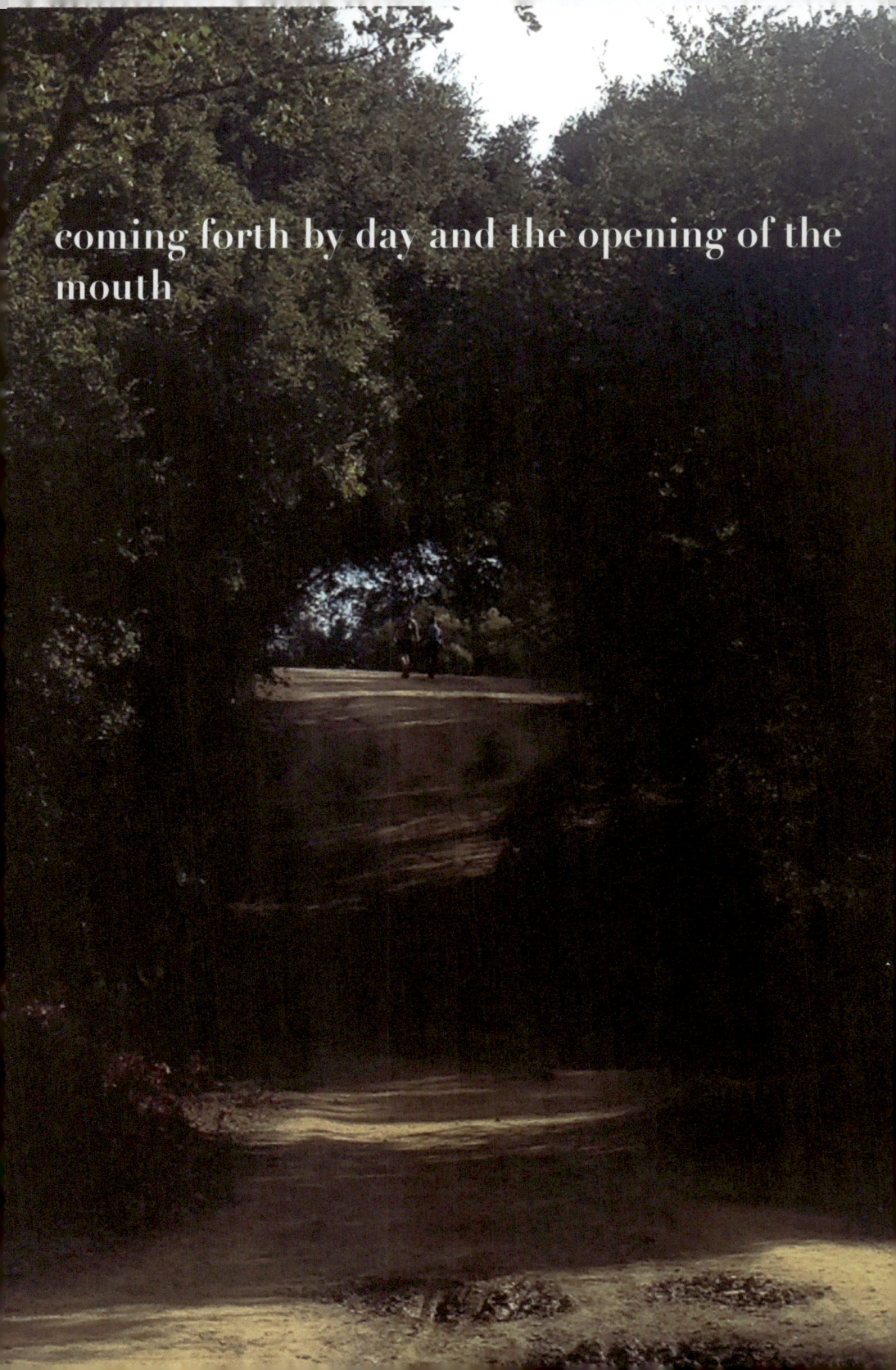

coming forth by day and the opening of the mouth

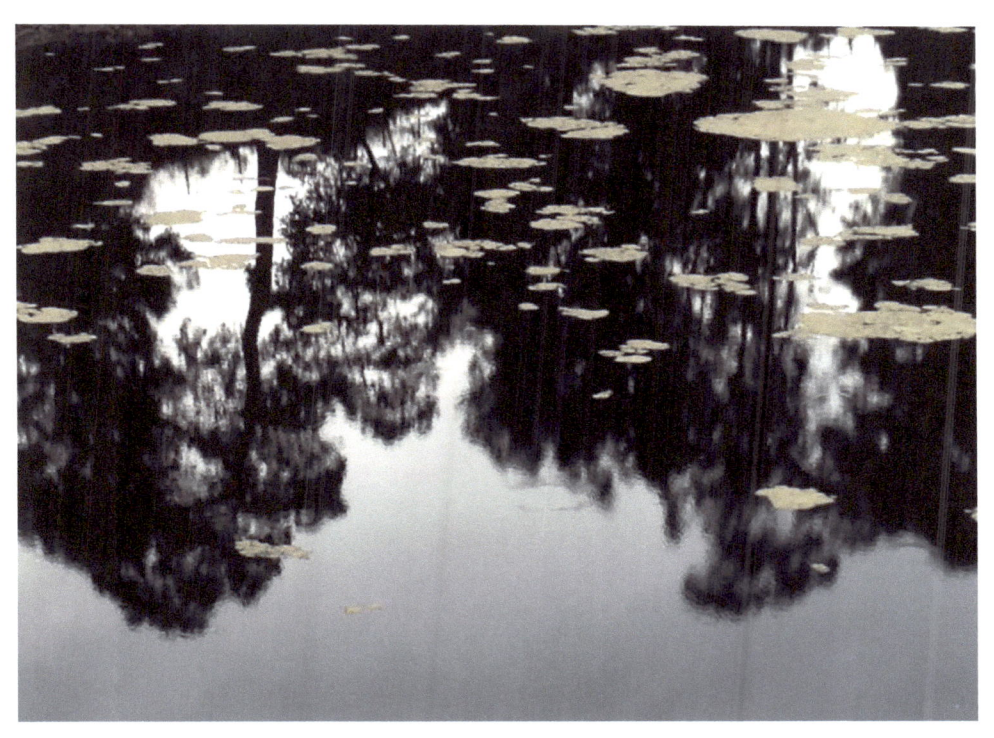

to the wet dark and low

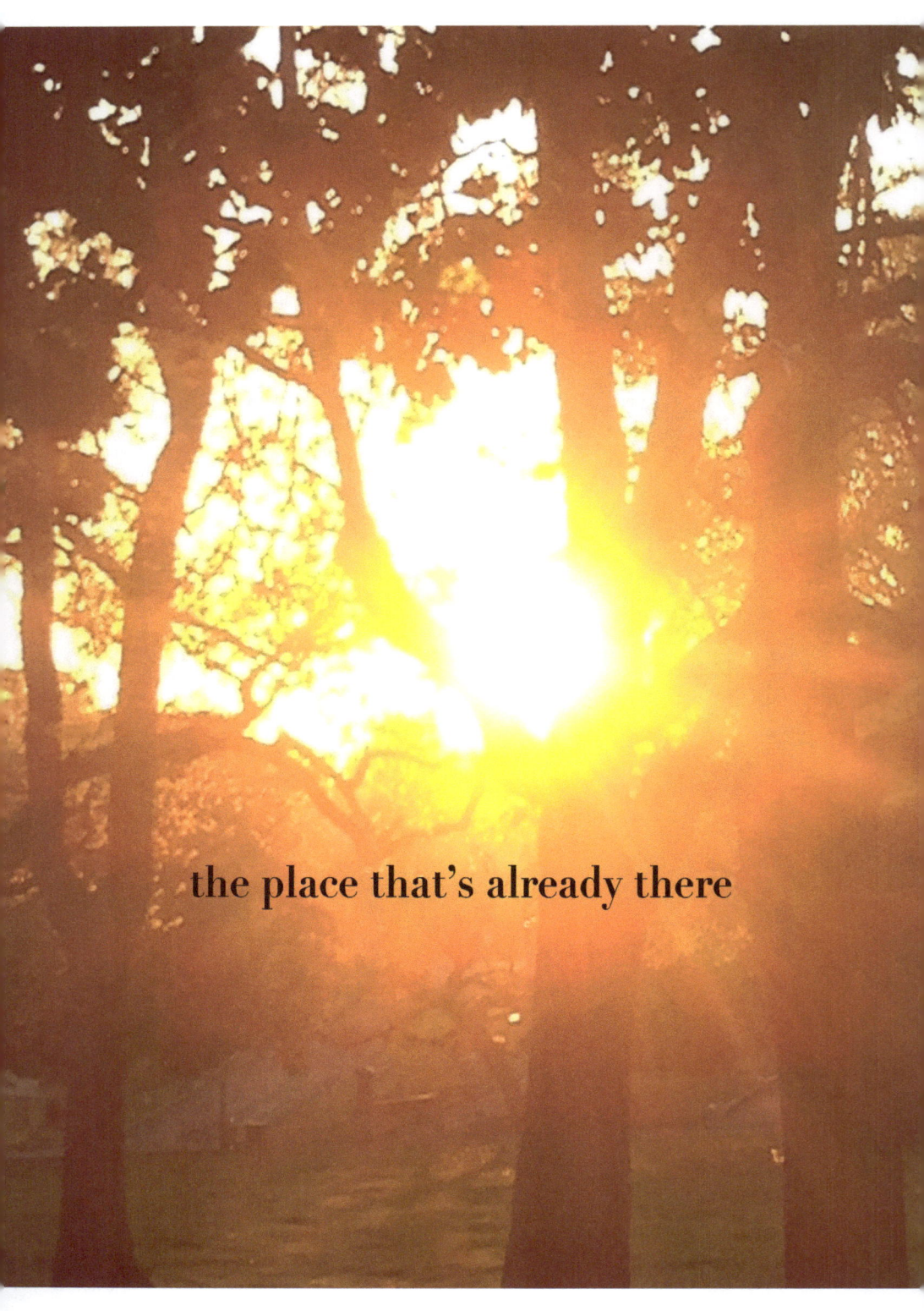

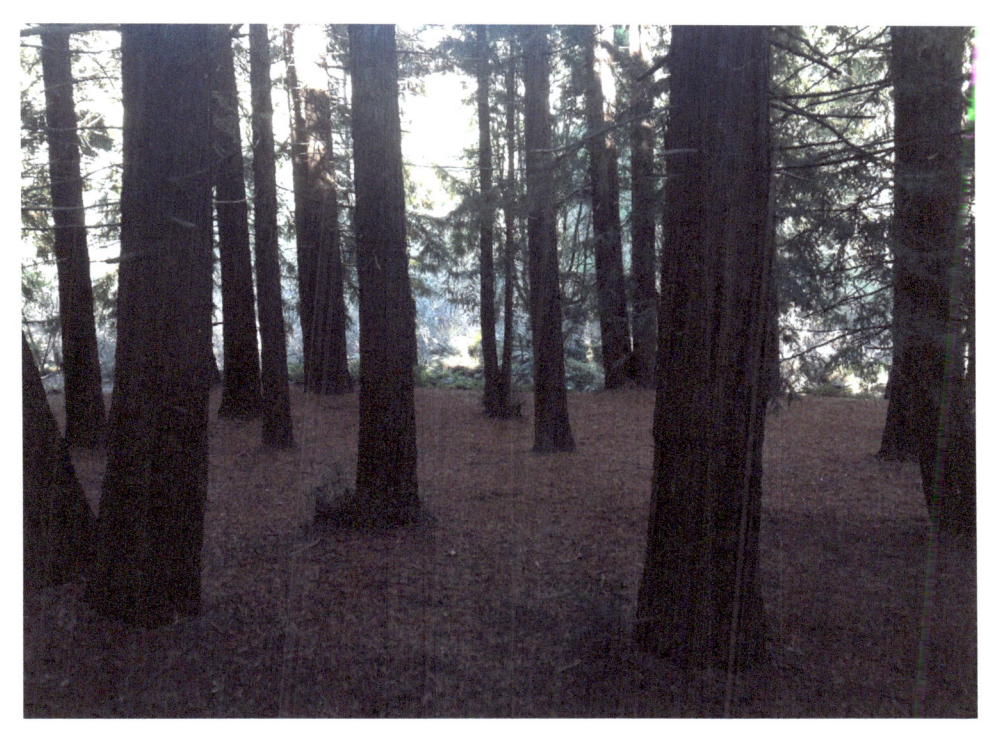

in the heart of the redwood grove

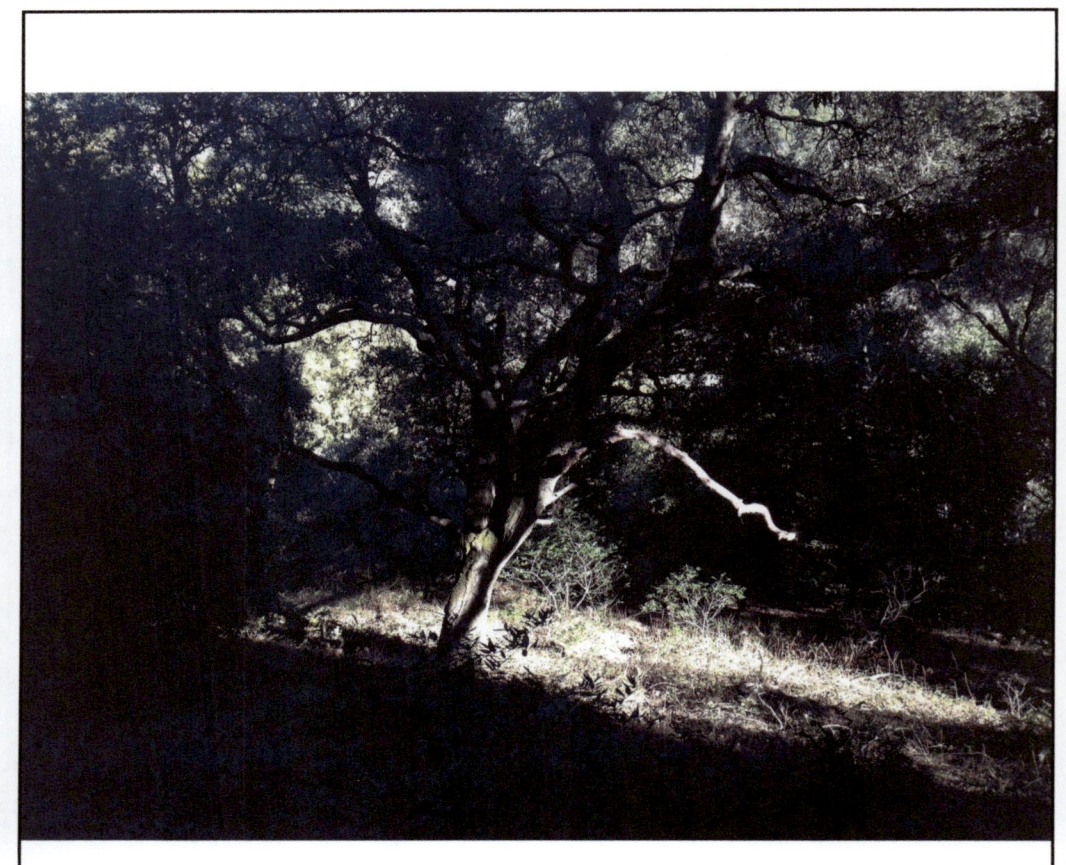

at the edge of the forest

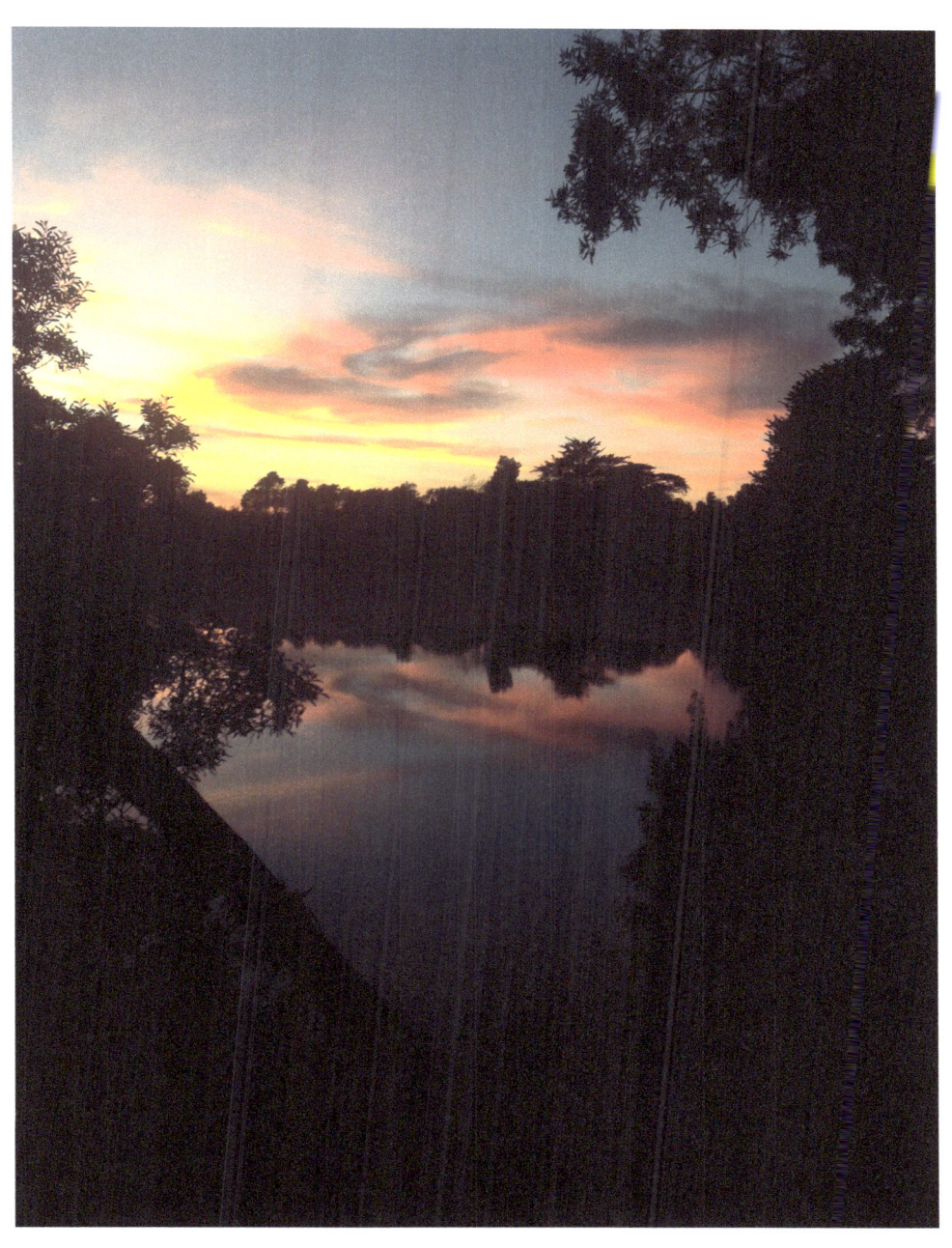

where golden snakes and
minnows swim

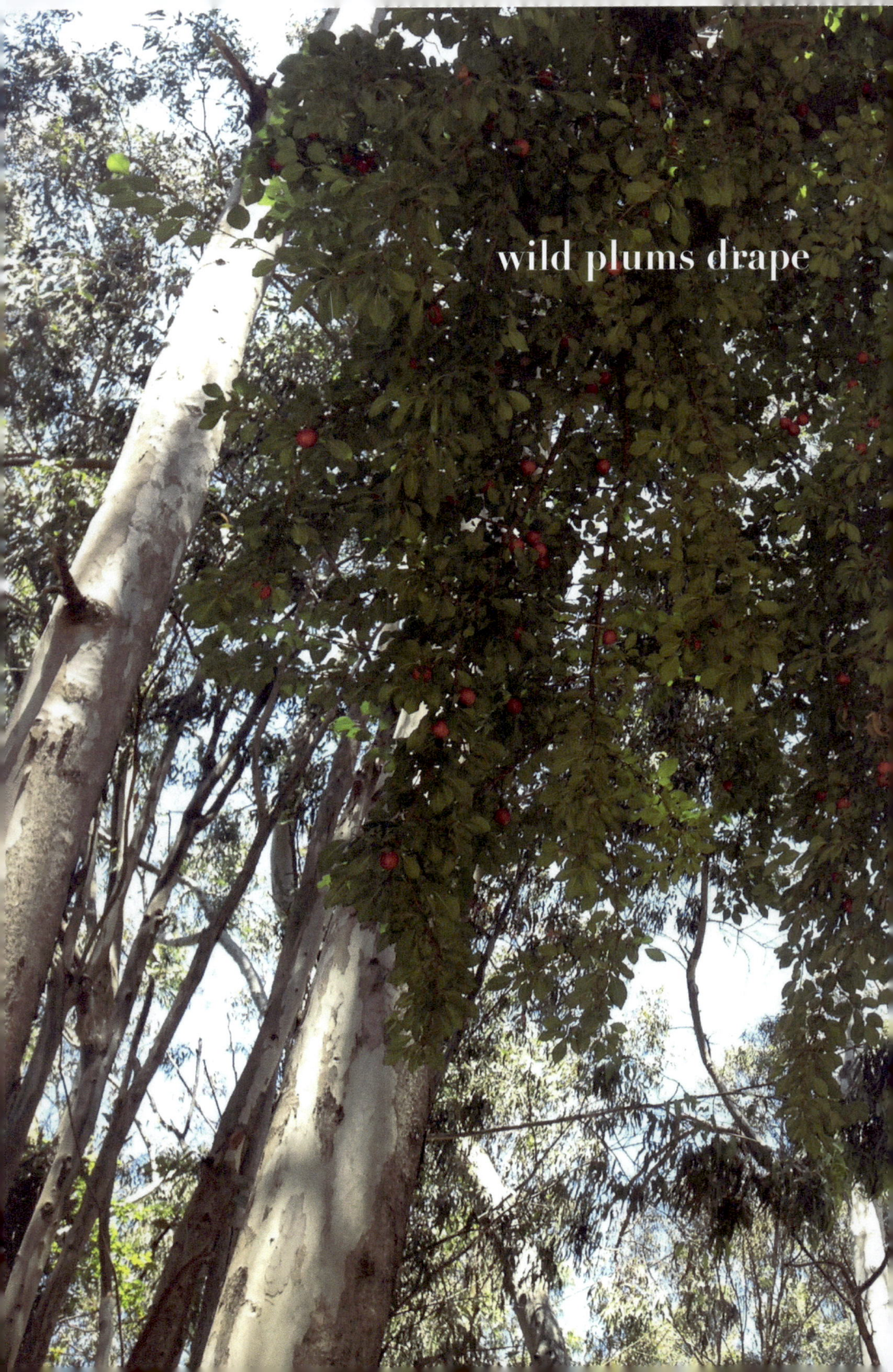
wild plums drape

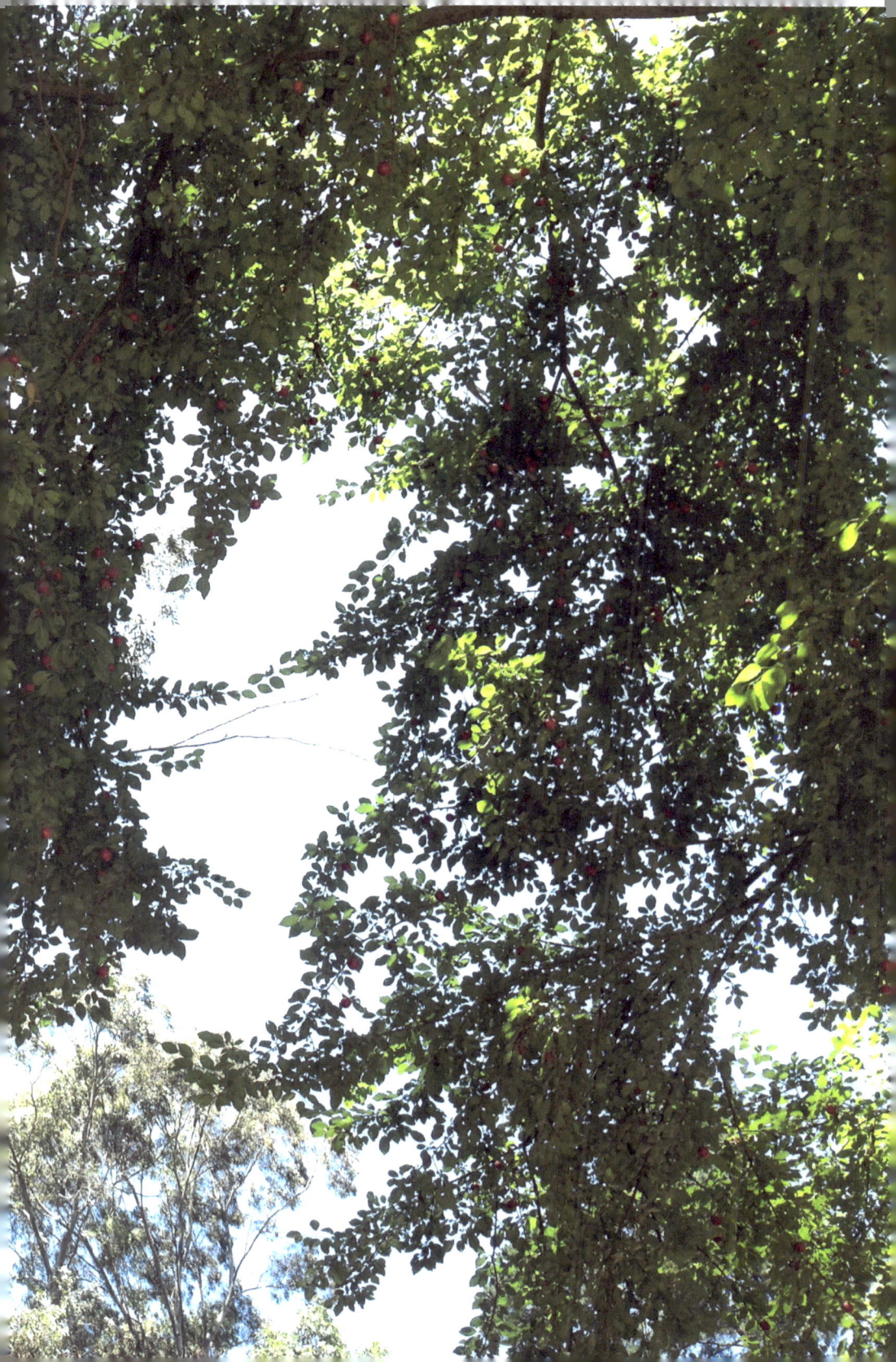

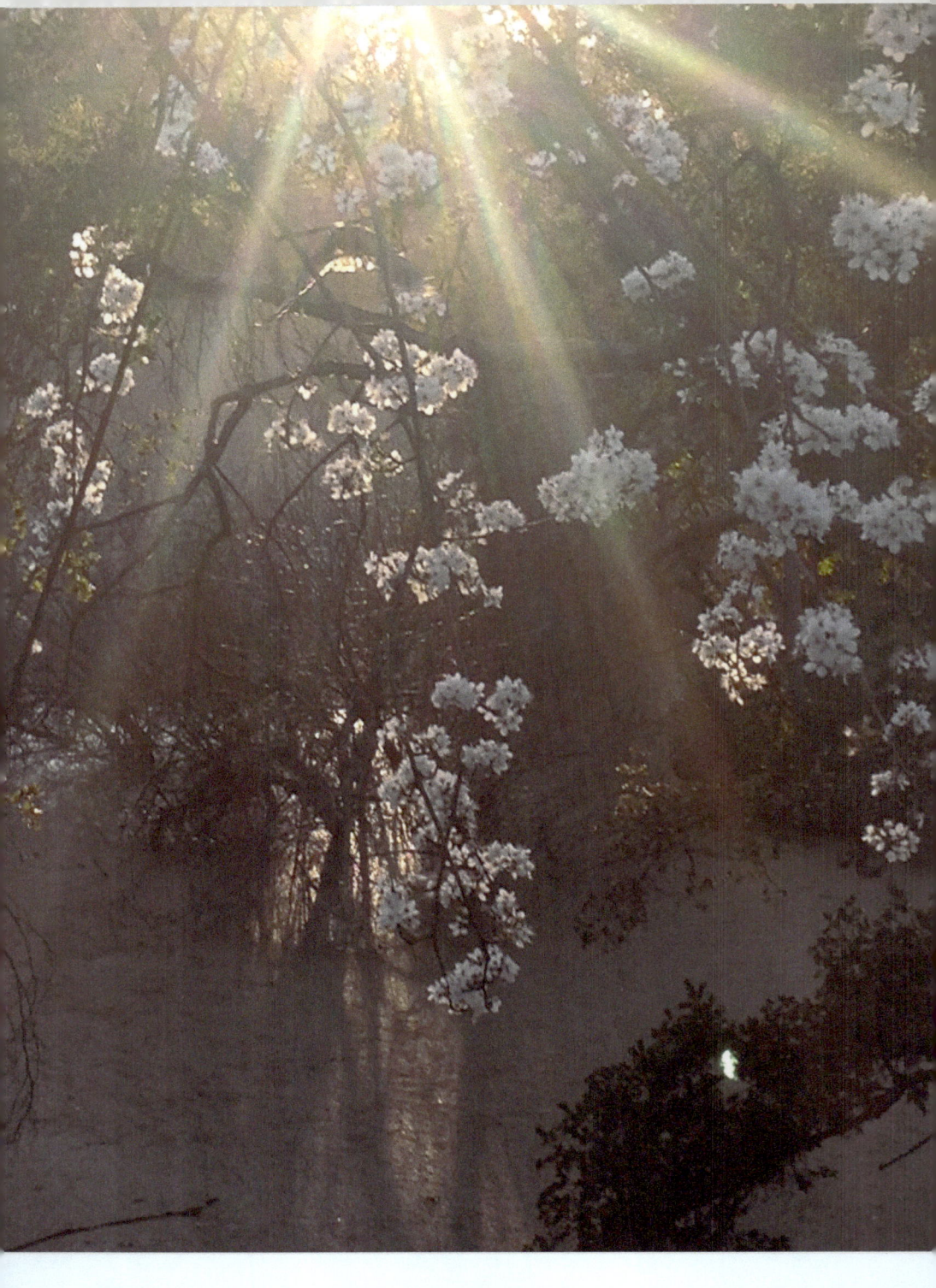

in the flicker – of the flicker (dark is first light)

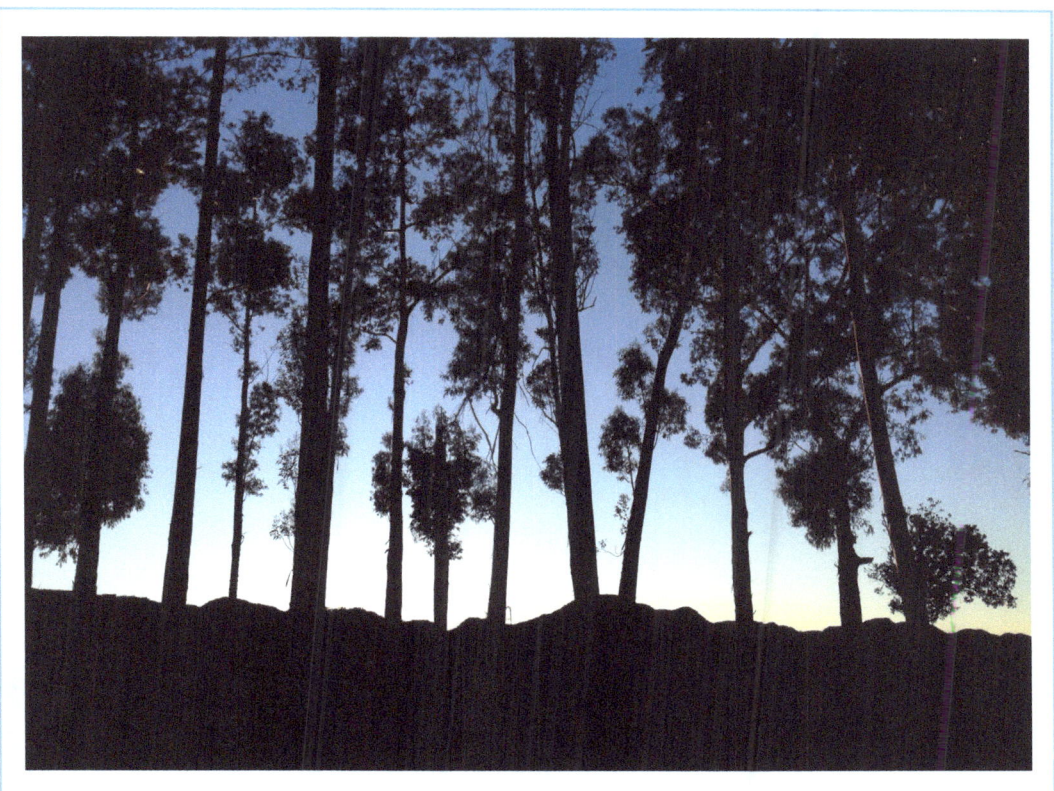

the idea of twilight in the present realm

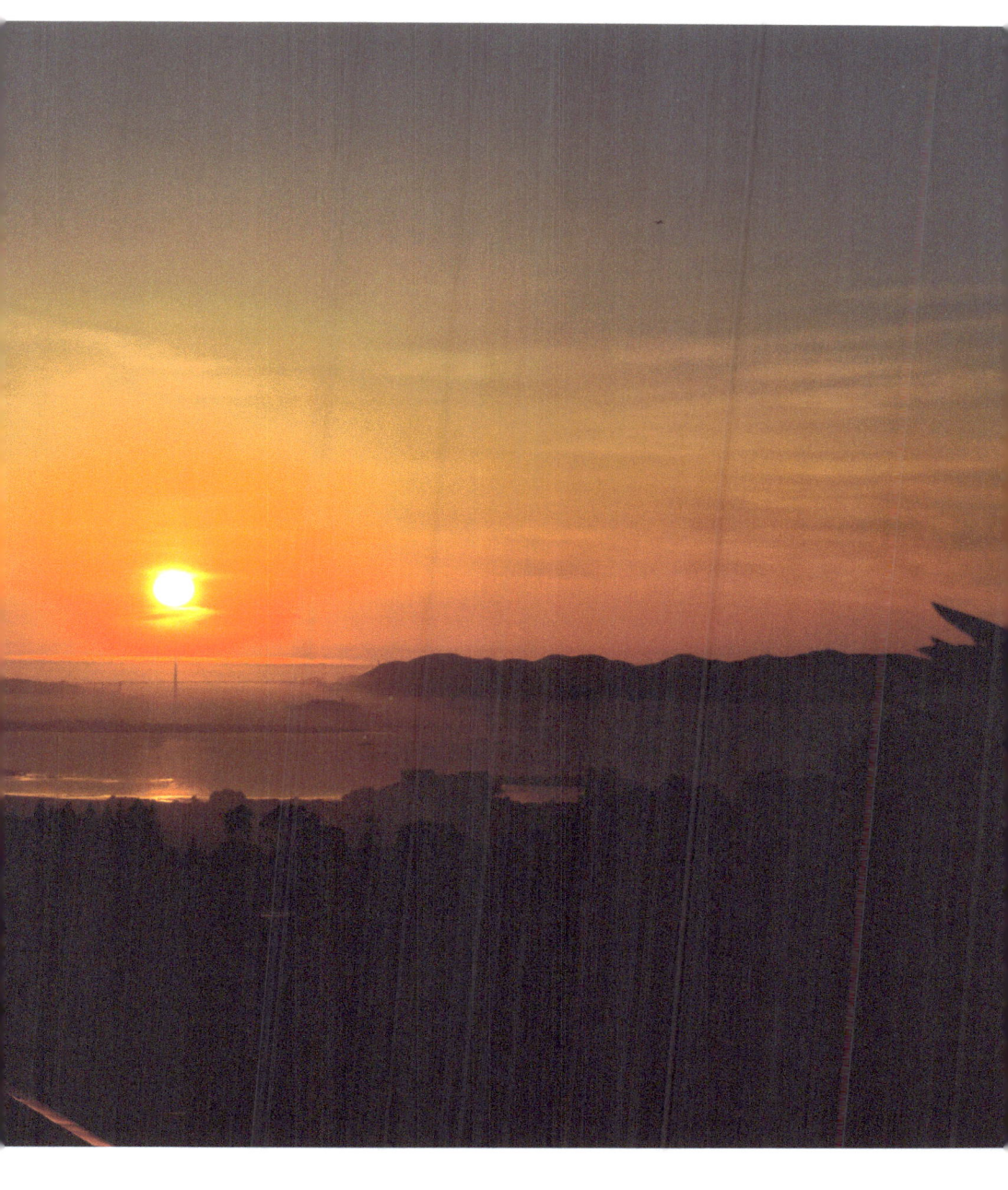

and you chasing the golden ball

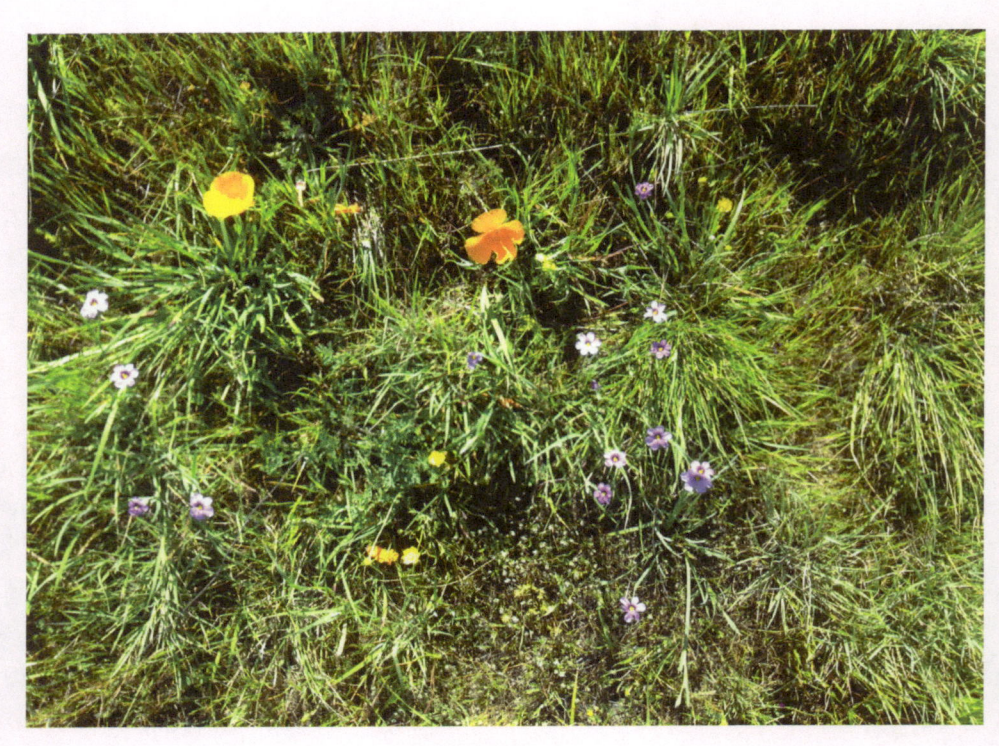

through an immense world of delight

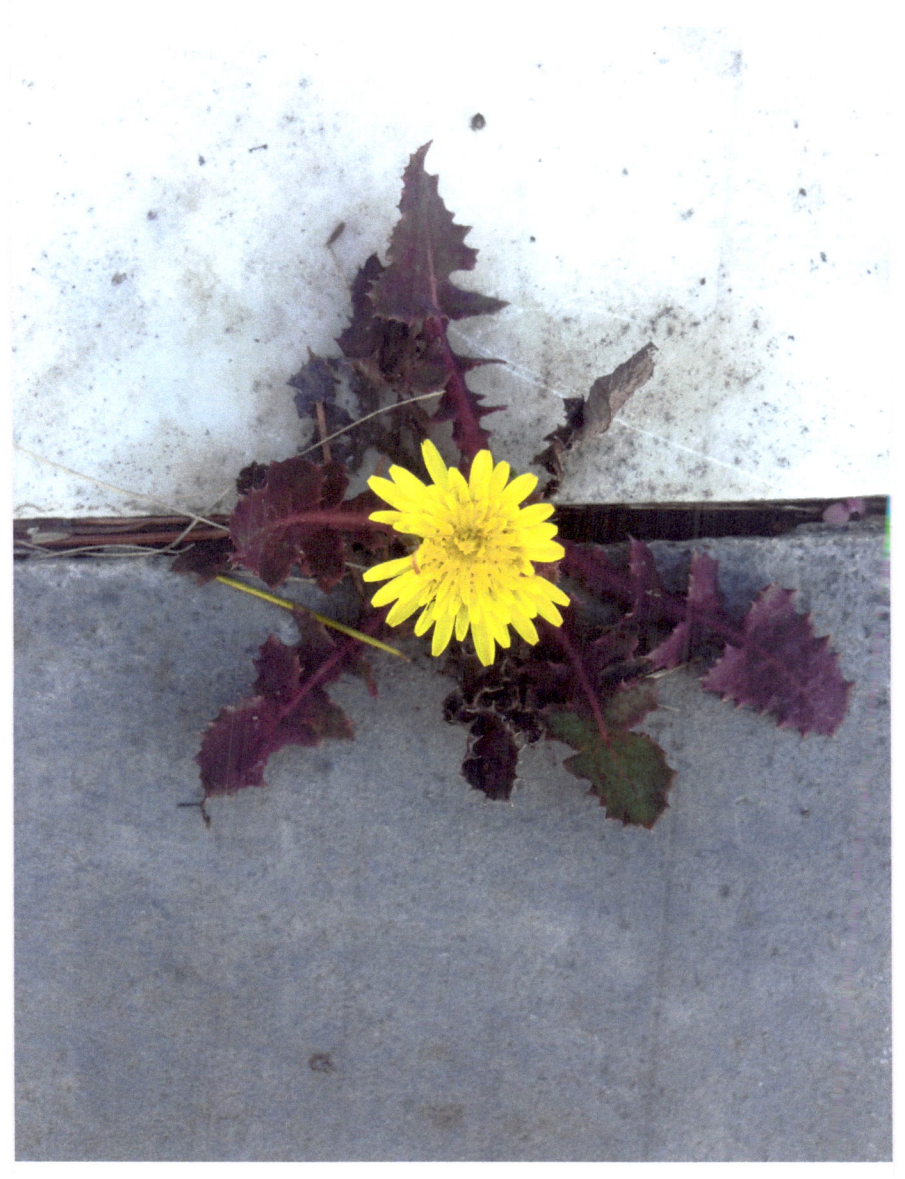

that falls between spheres

Coming Forth by Day
Sissel Kardel

Layout and design by B Taylor

BETA COPY 10012016
ISBN 978-1-943905-06-05

Crosby Street Press © 2016
354 Bowery #3
New York, NY 10012
http://www.crosbystreetpress.org

www.ingramcontent.com/pod-product-compliance
Lightning Source LLC
Chambersburg PA
CBHW040244220526
45473CB00001B/368